HOW TO TALK TO YOUR BOSS LIKE A BOSS

A Definitive Guide to Master the Art of Talking to Your Boss and Learn How to Get What You Want

Leonard L. Walker

Seven Suns Book Press

Copyright © 2021 by Leonard L. Walker – All rights reserved.

The content contained within this book may not be reproduced, duplicated, or transmitted without direct written permission from the author or the publisher.

Under no circumstances will any blame or legal responsibility be held against the publisher or author for any damages, reparation, or monetary loss due to the information contained within this book, either directly or indirectly.

Legal Notice:

This book is copyright protected. It is only for personal use. You cannot amend, distribute, sell, use, quote or paraphrase any part, or the content within this book, without the consent of the author or publisher.

Disclaimer Notice:

Please note the information contained within this document is for educational and entertainment purposes only. All effort has been executed to present accurate, up to date, reliable, complete information. No warranties of any kind are declared or implied. Readers acknowledge that the author is not engaged in the rendering of legal, financial, medical or professional advice. The content within this book has been derived from various sources. Please consult a licensed professional before attempting any techniques outlined in this book.

By reading this document, the reader agrees that under no circumstances is the author responsible for any losses, direct or indirect that are incurred as a result of the use of the information contained within this document, including, but not limited to, errors, omissions, or inaccuracies.

I want to dedicate this book to all the people in the world who are trying their hardest and pushing themselves every day. This dedication page is for everyone who needs help but is still giving it their all. To those who go into work every day with a smile on their face even if they don't feel like it because someone else needs them.

To my co-workers, family, and friends - may we always be there for each other when times get tough! I hope this book will help everyone with your career, so that you can make a difference for your family at home.

Contents

How this Book is Structured   I

Preface   II

1. Part I   1

2. Introduction   2

3. Why is it Important to Master the Skill of Talking to Your Boss?   3

4. Boss vs Employee: Are We All Equal?   4

5. Effective Communication–Getting What You Really Want   5

6. Negotiating With Your Boss   7

7. How to Fix Your Fear of Talking to Your Boss   9

8. Setting and Matching the Right Expectation   11

9. Be Confident in Front of Your Boss   12

10. How to Talk So Your Boss Will Listen   14

11. How to Stay Focused on What You Really Want When 16

Speaking with Your Boss

12. The Art of Persuasively Speaking to Your Boss — 19

13. How to Tell My Boss to Act and Talk Respectfully to Me — 22

14. How to Talk to Your Boss When You Disagree — 24

15. How to Stand Up Against an Unreasonable Boss — 27

16. Knowing When is the Perfect Time to Speak with Your Boss — 29

17. Build a Strong Relationship with Your Boss That Will Help You in the Future — 32

18. How to Make Your Boss Fall in Love with You — 34

19. Don't Talk to Your Boss Like You're Talking to a Friend — 37

20. Concluding Part I — 42

21. Part II — 44

22. How to Handle Difficult Conversations with the Boss in Different Situations — 45

23. When the Problem lies with Your Boss — 48

24. How to Talk to Your Boss About His Behavior That Displeases You — 49

25. How to Talk to Your Boss When They are Wrong — 52

26. How to Talk to Your Boss About a Problem that Lies with Him — 54

27. How Do You Tell Your Boss That They're a Bad Communicator — 57

28. How Do You Confront a Trash Talking Boss — 59

29. It Can Be Tricky to Handle Workplace Related Topic — 61

30. How to Talk to Your Boss About Toxic Co-workers — 62

31. How to Talk to Your Boss When You Are Unhappy at Work — 64

32. How to Talk to Your Boss That You are Overworked or Just Too Busy — 67

33. How to Talk to Your Boss About Shifting Responsibilities — 69

34. How to Talk to Your Boss When You Messed Up — 72

35. How to Talk to Your Boss and Convince Them to Let You Work Remotely — 74

36. Career Related Topics — 76

37. How to Talk to Your Boss When You're Underperforming — 77

38. How to Talk to Your Boss About Burnout — 80

39. How to Talk to Your Boss When You Feel Undervalued at Work — 83

40. How to Talk to Your Boss About Career Growth — 87

41. How to Ask Your Boss for a Promotion — 90

42. How to Ask Your Boss for a Pay Raise — 94

43. How to Talk to Your Boss About Quitting — 98

44. Personal Related Topics — 102

45. How to Talk to Your Boss About A Personal Issue That Persists At Work — 103

46. How to Speak with Your Boss about Work Life Balance — 106

47. How to Talk to Your Boss about Work Related Stress — 109

48. How to Talk to Your Boss About Your Work Anxiety — 112

49. How to Talk to Your Boss About Your Mental Health — 116

50. How to Talk to Your Boss If You're Struggling — 118

51. How to Tell Your Boss You're Unhappy at Work — 122

52. How to Tell Your Boss You're Pregnant — 124

53. Closing Chapter — 127

Author Note — 130

Editor Note — 132

How this Book is Structured

IN PART I OF this book, I will highlight several important basic communication skills that I think you should pick up if you want to have an effective communication with your boss. You will learn how to be confident when you are talking to your boss, how to set expectation in the conversation as well as how to handle a difficult conversation with them. And the most important of all, I will show you how to fix the fear of talking to them.

In Part II of this book, I will highlight the common scenarios where you may need to talk to your boss, and I will also share actionable steps so that you can find the best way to handle it. Some scenarios may not apply to you just yet, but I will encourage you to read them so you will know how to react when it happens.

PREFACE

I used to be afraid when speaking with my boss, so I would often let myself accept what they gave without asking for anything. I had a lot of trouble being assertive at work until the time came that everyone else needed and requested my skills - but not by management. It seems like no matter what I said or did; they wanted nothing to do with me; every time they'd ask for help or direction, all I got in return was "we'll let you know".

Being young and new to this working world, and anxious about rocking the boat too much and getting myself fired before my one-year mark (thank God), I sought advice from friends on how to survive in this harsh office environment.

They had some excellent advice for me, but the two most important pieces which I picked up were these: first, find out what your boss is looking for and then communicate it to them. Second, be sure that you're asking confidently; don't just ask a question like "should I do this?" or "may I do this?", which can come across as hesitant.

This looked way too simple and my first reaction was, "is that all?" But I did not question these, and I was so glad to have these pieces of advice because they made the workday much easier, and I survived for some 20 years later!

The first few years were really difficult, and I struggled. I couldn't contribute to the team as much NOT because I lacked experience but because it's common to have toxic colleagues around who just wasted time to sabotage you.

I'm sure that you can relate to how hard it is to be in this office environment and your only source of lifeline is none other than your immediate boss. And that's where the next problem comes in - how do you even talk to your boss about conflicts?

These problems are just a drop in the ocean. The key to a successful career is not simply about how much you can contribute to your company, but how well you can survive in the organisation and take care of business long enough within your company that will allow you the opportunity to contribute where your value is recognized and rewarded.

I've been in the workforce for over twenty years and counting and I have learned that I need to take charge of my own career progression. I know what areas to research, which leads should be pursued, and when I need an update from a manager. I learned to demand things without being demanding and make requests instead of demands because you're more likely to get them taken care of by your boss if they're phrased this way.

Anyone can achieve all that if you know the right way. I think you can almost guess it correctly; the right way is simply knowing how to talk to your boss and get what you want! There are ways you can learn on how to approach your boss to get what you want by knowing which things they will say yes and no to.

I have coached many people and served as a mentor to a few others who have been through the same tiresome journey that I did when I first started out in the workforce. This is a very common problem for those who are on the verge of leaving because they just can't take it anymore.

I wrote this book because I want to reach out to more people who don't know me personally, and I hope to help this group of people who are still struggling to find the right way in which they can get what they want from their boss while still respecting them and not making it feel you are demanding things.

The tips and advice I shared in this book are based on over 20 years of experience working with different bosses and different colleagues and I shared own experiences as well as what worked best for me when I was an employee who was always looking for ways trying to get ahead in my career.

To be honest, and it may sound strange, I really hope that you don't need to read this book because that would probably mean that you are doing well. Otherwise, if you belong to the following few categories below, I'm very sure that this could be the best basic book to help you survive the harsh working world, or at least survive in the first few years of your career.

This book will be useful to you if:

1. You're new to the workforce, and you don't know how to communicate with your boss, or maybe you've been working for a while but have never learned how to talk to your boss.
2. You are learning how to survive in a toxic environment and want to learn how to talk to your boss about conflicts.
3. You need help with talking to your boss about things like pay raises, flexible hours or asking for more training.
4. You want to learn how to speak up for yourself at work without getting fired.
5. You just want to know how to talk to your boss and get what you want.

PART I

INTRODUCTION

HOW DO YOU TALK to your boss and get what you want? It is a question that many of us struggle with. We are often afraid to ask for things we really need in fear of being seen as too demanding or difficult, but the truth is that if you do not make your needs clear, it will be impossible for them to meet them! In this book, I will share tips on how to figure out what you really need from the boss and how best to communicate those needs so they can help. The tips shared emphasize certain consideration that one need to have and be mindful of before they speak with their bosses and get what they want when it comes time for these conversations.

I know and trust me; I understand it has never been a good feeling to be in a position where you have got to talk to your boss about something. Whether it is a raise, a responsibility change, or anything else that will impact your life or your career within the company, there are many ways for how this conversation can go wrong, and I will try to help you minimize the chances of that from happening.

Why is it Important to Master the Skill of Talking to Your Boss?

IT IS AN ESSENTIAL life skill for every person out there! When you master this crucial speaking skill set, not only does it make things easier for yourself when making requests but also helps build relationships with those around you as well, since everyone needs someone on his or her side at work. Mastering the art of speaking to your boss effectively is one of the most important skill you need to get what you want. For some, there are few opportunities of speaking with their bosses and getting what they wanted but when the time comes, you have to grab it and not fumble. Many people struggled at this crucial moment.

Hopefully, by the end of this book, you will learn how to avoid the common pitfalls of talking with your boss, and you will learn how to control your own communications, grow in confidence when dealing with a difficult boss or any other communication challenges you may encounter on your career path.

Take a breather here and consider what I'd just said.

And when you are ready, let us begin.

Boss vs Employee: Are We All Equal?

THE RELATIONSHIP BETWEEN BOSS and employee is one that should be treated with a high degree of respect. The order of the hierarchy in this relationship dictates how each person behaves. For example, when an employee feels like they need to approach their boss for something, it is important that you should set a meeting and speak out in person and not just by emailing. Likewise, a boss should not abruptly interrupt an employee when they are in the middle of conversation, or worse condescendingly.

For the betterment of both employees and bosses, there should be mutual respect and understanding for an effective communication to take place when you are talking to your boss. These should be set in place so you can really convey and achieve what you really want amicably.

Why is it Important to Master the Skill of Talking to Your Boss?

IT IS AN ESSENTIAL life skill for every person out there! When you master this crucial speaking skill set, not only does it make things easier for yourself when making requests but also helps build relationships with those around you as well, since everyone needs someone on his or her side at work. Mastering the art of speaking to your boss effectively is one of the most important skill you need to get what you want. For some, there are few opportunities of speaking with their bosses and getting what they wanted but when the time comes, you have to grab it and not fumble. Many people struggled at this crucial moment.

Hopefully, by the end of this book, you will learn how to avoid the common pitfalls of talking with your boss, and you will learn how to control your own communications, grow in confidence when dealing with a difficult boss or any other communication challenges you may encounter on your career path.

Take a breather here and consider what I'd just said.

And when you are ready, let us begin.

Boss vs Employee: Are We All Equal?

THE RELATIONSHIP BETWEEN BOSS and employee is one that should be treated with a high degree of respect. The order of the hierarchy in this relationship dictates how each person behaves. For example, when an employee feels like they need to approach their boss for something, it is important that you should set a meeting and speak out in person and not just by emailing. Likewise, a boss should not abruptly interrupt an employee when they are in the middle of conversation, or worse condescendingly.

For the betterment of both employees and bosses, there should be mutual respect and understanding for an effective communication to take place when you are talking to your boss. These should be set in place so you can really convey and achieve what you really want amicably.

Effective Communication—Getting What You Really Want

HOW DO YOU TELL your boss what you really want? If you want to communicate with your boss effectively and advance your career, it is the skill of approaching your boss that is key. Communicating with them can sometimes be difficult because they have certain expectations that differ from yours... but if you know what they are looking for, this will make it easier.

After all, your boss still holds the key to your advancement within your company. A simple 5 steps to ensure a smooth review or feedback session is:

1. Figure out what you want and write it down: You need to have a clear understanding of what it is you want in order for him to be able to provide feedback on these areas. Your goal must be clear so that it will not become a wasted or meaningless feedback session.

2. Be specific and be clear about what you want and why it's important to you: Be specific about what you want. If you are trying to say something and it's not working, try going more in-depth. The more details you provide, the more feedback you will receive in return.

3. Have a meeting with your boss to discuss what you want: Be confident, but not aggressive - Be confident in what you believe and be clear about the importance of it being discussed. It is important

not to come off aggressive because that may scare him away from talking further with you on this topic.

4. Make sure that the timing is right- don't do it when they're busy or in a foul mood: When you are having this meeting, make sure it's not when they are busy or in a grim mood. If that is the case and you still want to talk with them about this topic, try setting up another time for later on- so long as it doesn't take too long to discuss what needs to be discussed.

5. Be prepared for a "no" answer: Even though you're confident in what you want to discuss, you need to be prepared for a "no" answer. You may have had many discussions about this topic and still not get the desired result. There are two reasons that could happen: either he doesn't think it's important or he does not see how your idea will work. That is why it is important that you plan out your conversation and prepare how to handle his questions or replies. It is like your first interview with him, except that it is not.

Negotiating With Your Boss

IF YOU ARE LOOKING for ways to improve your life at work, one of the best things that you can do is learn how to negotiate with your boss. Negotiating isn't a dirty word, and it doesn't have to be hard either. In the workplace, the boss usually holds all the cards. It is important to know how to negotiate with your boss so that you can get what you want in a negotiation. Sometimes you may not get all. But know your bottom line and negotiate from the top down, so that at the end of the day, you will still get something out of the negotiation.

I know it is easier said than done. How many times have you been in a meeting with your boss and thought, "I should have negotiated for more." We're sure it happens to everyone, me included. Countless times! But the more I negotiate (even for the smallest thing), the better and natural I become. It's no secret that negotiation is an important part of business, and yes, even at work! If you don't know how to negotiate, then you could be missing out on valuable opportunities for advancement or pay increases!

Below are some quick tips that worked for me, and that will teach you the basics about negotiating with your boss so that you can get what YOU want!

1. Know what they want and why they want it: If your boss wants something from you, then there should be some reasoning behind it. You need to find out what their desired outcome is so that this

can affect how you approach negotiations. If you know and can give them what they want, this could be the bargaining chip to get what YOU want.

Example scenario:
I would like more flexibility with my schedule, and an increase in pay so that I am compensated for what I bring into work every day. But before negotiating these things, we need to figure out what and why he wants something from me! He probably wants someone who is reliable and prepared at all times, which is something else that needs consideration during negotiations. Knowing this, I will angle my negotiation that focuses more on how I can get the work done in a more efficient manner without compromising on quality. I will give him what he wants, and chances are I'm likely to get what I want too!

2. Think about the alternatives: When looking at different options, think about which one would be best for both parties involved in the negotiation. There may not be a perfect solution, but if there is a suitable compromise suggestion or solution on the table, it could be the best outcome for both parties.

3. Consider their leverage: What is your boss's position in the company? How much can they offer to you? A good negotiator will know when it's time to make a trade. Knowing their capacity on how much the boss can grant you will make the negotiation easier. For example, can they grant you a 30% pay raise? Or the maximum that they can grant you is only a 7% pay raise? You get the point.

To summarize the negotiation process in one liner: be aware of what THEY want because this could help you get WHAT YOU WANT!

How to Fix Your Fear of Talking to Your Boss

WHAT SEEMS TO BE one of the most common problems is a fear of talking to their boss. Many gave up just by having the thought of it and didn't even try. Their fear can stem from many factors, including the dread of being reprimanded or maybe even fired because they were too vocal about something. They see the boss as semi-god and their words as absolute. They imagine the boss to be rejecting whatever request they made.

Let me tell you, it is not true, and I don't want you to fall into this sinking thought. The bosses, or your direct supervisors, are just like you and me, a normal human being. No matter what the primary reason may be, there are ways one can go about fixing their problem, so communication becomes easier between them and their superiors. And if you are also struggling with this same fear, there are several tips that I will share with you now to help you overcome this mental obstacle. One thing is for sure- you need to practice and fix it before things get worse and progress stalls.

One simple technique includes communicating more often, saying what needs to be said instead of worrying about who will react poorly, coming up with strategies on how not to have conversations derailed by aggressive comments/responses. Don't always imagine the worst, and always prepare your conversation.

A few other tips that might also help:

1. You need to be calm when you talk to your boss and do it in a way that ensures your thoughts and message get sent. Act like talking with another colleague rather than before an authoritative boss, so you are not afraid of talking about what's on your mind. It may not be entirely foolproof; it will at least help you calm down and start with a rational mind.

2. Figure out what you want to say and prepare ahead of the conversation. Get a clear understanding of what you want out of the conversation and practice your speech in front of a mirror or with a friend. This is important, so you have a clear direction of what to talk about and how to voice your thoughts. Thinking for some time beforehand will also help keep the conversation flowing as well as make it easier for both parties involved in the conversation.

3. For you to communicate your thoughts effectively, it's important for you to keep it short and simple and get every word out clearly and precisely. You also want them to understand the message that you are trying to deliver, so make sure you do not miss out on anything important when responding accordingly.

4. Prepare yourself for your boss's probable reactions when you speak to them. Some topics that are slightly touchy can become uncomfortable when you are speaking to your boss. It might be tempting for you to get defensive or angry, but this will most likely lead to a more difficult conversation and make it even more unpleasant. Before talking with your boss about any sensitive topic, prepare yourself on how you will respond if they disagree.

Setting and Matching the Right Expectation

IF A TYPICALLY TIMID employee were to bring up an issue that needs to be addressed, it would set the expectation that the boss will need to consider this issue seriously because this comes from an employee who was usually quiet. Likewise, if the employee is typically aggressive and suddenly meek, it would set the expectation that they are no longer interested in addressing this issue at all.

Knowing what the expectation is will allow you to approach it more appropriately, so it does not confuse your boss or lead them to believe that you agree with something which is not your intention.

Many people find managing their boss' expectations to be a challenge. And yet, it remains one of the most important skills for ensuring a conducive work environment with a smooth and successful career. That's why I'm emphasizing to you now that setting and matching expectations with your boss is very important.

BE CONFIDENT IN FRONT OF YOUR BOSS

SOME OF YOU MAY never have had the chance to talk to your supervisors about how well you're doing or what you can improve on. It's normal for some people to feel nervous when trying to speak with them. But If you are confident enough to speak your mind, this will show potential employers that you voice your opinions and use initiative. This complements the negotiation skill that we touched on earlier.

There are a few tactics you can use to boost your confidence and negotiate with your boss better. Again, all these need practice, practice and more practice!

1. Make sure you know your stuff: The way you will deliver your message and the right choice of words will depend on how well you know the subject. Speaking with confidence and conviction will more likely produce an outcome that is beneficial to you, or at least has a higher chance of meeting your aim. If you can't answer a question that was posed to you, don't even think of bluffing your way through because you may get found out and it will reduce your credibility, and you may find it difficult to get back on track.

2. Speak slowly and use simple words: The whole idea here is to pass on the correct message in the simplest and shortest way possible. It may seem counterintuitive, but if you can't get your point across in fewer words and sentences, then it's usually because what you are trying to say is too complicated.

3. Be prepared: Just doing some homework beforehand will give you the ability to keep the conversation flowing and focus on the end goal. Remember your aim for this meeting and do not let your boss get sidetracked or digressed.

How to Talk So Your Boss Will Listen

TALKING TO YOUR BOSS can be difficult, and it's easy for them not to listen. Many of them find it hard because they think about what will happen when things don't go well. They fear they might lose their job if the approach is wrong, but I can tell you from my experience, it is very unlikely.

If you are still worried, there are ways around this! There are many simple tips that you can pick up and know that using those techniques won't make anything worse than how they already were before - in fact, a few different approaches may even get better results! So you really have nothing to lose and everything to gain!

Here are a few simple tips that might work for you:

1. Be concise. Make sure to only talk about what is important and make the point as quickly as possible while still working on all the necessary information. This makes it easier for your boss to understand you and also gives them less opportunity to interrupt or change topics.

2. Keep cool even when things aren't going well or when people disagree with one another. Sometimes, this can be difficult, but if you stay calm, then it's more likely that they'll listen to what you have to say and take on board how much effort you've put into being heard before dismissing anything.

3. Only talk about what's important at that moment. This will allow them to stick with one topic and not feel overwhelmed or like it's an overwhelming task. Straight to the point and make it simple to understand and evaluate.

4. Watch your tonality. If needed, use a calm tone and don't raise your voice even when you are angry. Keep it that way throughout the entire conversation and ensuring that it stays on course by getting to what you want said as quickly as possible.

5. Be clear about why this conversation is important and be very specific about the raised issues when giving examples or describing how it relates to others involved.

6. If there is something that you don't know how to say without offending them or making them think less of you, try using short phrases such as "I would love for us both to be happy" or "I'd really appreciate it if we could work together on this." This will show respect and encourage more open communication from their end.

7. Finish with an action plan that outlines the steps going forward so you have something you can put into practice immediately, something that your boss agreed on. This will make them more likely to listen closely since they'll know you're not just talking for no reason - now there's a productive end goal at hand!

How to Stay Focused on What You Really Want When Speaking with Your Boss

ANOTHER COMMON PROBLEM THAT many people didn't realize is they lose sight of what they want to achieve in the conversation. Do you often spoke with your boss and then realize that you have gone off on a tangent? Do you want to make sure they know what you really want, but don't know how to communicate it effectively?

What you want to say is important. But how you say it can make all the difference in your success—both with your boss and on the job.

We all know how easy it is to get distracted when speaking with our boss. It's hard to stay focused on what you really want, and we often end up doing a lot of talking without actually getting anything done. It's easy for a conversation to go off track, especially when we're nervous or excited about what we have to share.

In my conversation with friends and ex-colleagues, I realized many of them cannot communicate with their boss because they feel inferior. This is a confidence issue. They assume their bosses are smarter than them, when in reality the bosses just want effective suggestions, not an empty opinion.

Communication is not just about you; it's also about the person who will listen to what you have to say and how they perceive your message. It does not matter if that individual has a unique background different from yours or a different opinion as long as they can get on board with where you're going, then it all works out in the end. From my experience, the boss will value more of a person who has the vision to drive the company forward.

Some people have trouble making a direct request with their boss and assume that the idea they suggested will be rejected. This leads them to stop talking or change the subject, which is usually ineffective in getting what you want.

I have 3 important tips that will help you stay focused on what you really want when speaking with your boss. Try it out and see if it works for you too.

1. Be clear about "why" this meeting is happening before diving into the specifics of "what." Know your end goal before speaking with your boss and know beforehand exactly what you want from this meeting so that when your boss asks, "what do you need?" or "what can I do for you?", you are ready to express your request - many get mental knocked out when they hear these questions.

2. Understand that there is a time and place for everything - don't speak out of turn - don't butt in just because you have something important to share; wait for the right timing in the meeting to provide input or ask questions. This may seem like common sense, but if we're too nervous or excited, our brains go off track, especially when we're nervous or excited about what we have to share. Because if you catch them at the wrong time, your boss may have to brush this conversation to another time - which can often be a big hit to your confidence of bringing up the topic again.

3. Use positive language - instead of negative phrases like "I don't think" or "perhaps," use affirmative words such as "yes" and "I'm

sure". This way, even if your boss doesn't agree, they know you believe in your idea. The confidence you portray in your conversation is important because it will help them take you seriously. This reinforces a firm impression of you and might just help you in your future conversation.

The Art of Persuasively Speaking to Your Boss

I BELIEVE THAT THE art of persuading your boss is a skill that every employee should learn. There are many benefits to being able to persuade others (especially your boss), which include increased job security and higher pay. If you want to be successful in the workplace, it's important that you know how to speak persuasively and convince your boss that you deserve what you're asking for.

I'm sure you'd been in a situation when your boss or management said no to something that you really wanted. You could have the best idea, but if they don't think it's a good one, then there's not much you can do about it. I was in that situation before, and I can never forget that feeling in my entire life. And worst, if you were like me, afraid to speak up and you worry about what your boss will think, and you don't want to rock the boat, then chances are you will face many disappointments. Period.

Now what if I tell you that sometimes speaking up is exactly what's needed? Yes, you heard it right. It can be that simple. From saying "no" when someone asks for an unreasonable favor, to telling your boss about a problem, there are many times when communicating with authority makes life so much easier.

There're a few techniques where you can go from a "no" to many "yeses". That requires you to master the art of persuasion. The art of persuasively speaking to your boss goes beyond just being convincing; it's also about understanding how bosses think and what they need from their employees so that you can speak their language and have a greater chance at success.

1. Be confident in your abilities and skills. Ask for what you want and explain why it's important to you and prepare your arguments for why you deserve them. If you are confident about your abilities, people will notice and recognize your skills. After all, confidence is contagious! You'll be surprised at how often people will say yes!

2. Create an emotional response. Understand that it's not just about you, but what is best for the company. Persuasion is the art of presenting your point in that direction, inciting no conflict to your request. You must be able to understand what's best for the company and create an emotional response without being too personal about it. When it is possible to have a win-win outcome, there's a high chance you may get what you want.

3. Practice what you are going to say until it sounds natural and persuasive. Develop and practice your delivery until it resonates with you. Listeners are more likely to be convinced if it sounds persuasive to you. After all, if you can't even convince yourself, then how are you going to convince others?

4. Establish a good rapport with your boss through verbal and nonverbal communication. Keep your head up, spine straightened, arms uncrossed and use open gestures to come across as confident when you speak. These will help establish the tone of voice that is smart without being aggressive or passive-aggressive so your boss trust what you say more easily. This, completes with a rehearsed delivery, will make your case even more compelling than before.

5. Offer to take responsibility for any potential consequences of implementing your solution. This will assure both you and your

boss that the plan is worth it.

All said, remember to keep your boss's personality in mind and speak accordingly. The tone of voice you use with different bosses will vary from being more casual and relaxed when speaking to a close friend or coworker to being very formal or even intimidating when addressing someone who is higher ranking than you are at work. If it's too complicated for you, just stay with a calm tone, and that should do the trick in most situation.

How to Tell My Boss to Act and Talk Respectfully to Me

THIS IS TRICKY, AND it's especially hard if you have a boss who behaves like he is one up above everyone else. I know that feeling, when people are condescending to us, it can be hard not to take their words personally. But the reality is, our reaction is usually less about what they say and more about how we feel about ourselves. Often, it is the sense of inferiority that causes the frustration and helplessness.

It's a real challenge because while we speak respectfully to our boss, we also need them to give it back to us - both in words and actions. So, what can you do when your boss won't treat you with respect? I'll share with you strategies on how you can be assertive without being aggressive.

1. Use a friendly tone of voice. The way we talk is a crucial part of how others treat us. A research study found that when employees acted rudely or had low energy during interactions, the boss was more likely to be dismissive and demeaning towards them. So, if you want your boss to respect you, show him some courtesy in both words and tone of voice.

2. Ask the boss to slow down when things get heated. This can happen pretty easily when we start being assertive with our bosses about mutual respect. Things can get out of hand easily. The more that you're forced to speak up for yourself, the less likely they are

going to keep going at you. Your best bet is still to keep things in control and tactfully break the momentum before the situation turned nasty.

3. When the boss gets angry and starts screaming at you, tell them to calm down or stop talking to you like that, or try to help by saying "It sounds like you are really mad." This will give them a chance to calm down for just a little while before they start again so that both of you can stay in control. It is important that you do not yell back and not to get defensive or lash out because anger won't solve anything! The key is to not react in anger or defensiveness and to always stay calm. Although sometimes being assertive can be the only way to handle an argumentative boss with disrespectful verbal abuse.

How to Talk to Your Boss When You Disagree

I AM SURE MANY of you have been in this situation before. You are at work and your boss is telling you how to do a certain thing. And as they talk, you don't agree with what they are saying. But how do you disagree professionally?

Being able to disagree with your boss is something few people can or willing to do. They do not want to risk getting into the boss' bad book. They do not want to be seen as going against the boss' idea. Whatever the reason, it can be difficult because you might not always see eye-to-eye, or your opinion may just differ from theirs. The ability and courage to disagree is a vital skill for anyone.

Most people might choose just to go along with what the boss says, but there are ways where you can respectfully disagree and voice your opinion too! You can disagree tactfully without offending them or getting into trouble while still respecting their authority!

1. The first thing you need to convince yourself is that it's okay not to always agree. Your opinion and thoughts are just as important, so speak up! You can voice any disagreement when the timing is appropriate and don't be afraid of being assertive if they ask for feedback or input from you.

2. Make sure that what you want them to know comes across clearly by speaking directly and respectfully about why you feel

differently than they do. Try using phrases like "I think" or "from my perspective." This allows space for a discussion without attacking their position right off the bat. It also makes it easier for both parties involved in an argument because nobody feels attacked - which will keep things more civil overall.

3. Don't be afraid of confrontation, but try not to attack them outright. Express your disagreement professionally. State why you feel differently and then ask for their input on how to solve the problem. This will allow them to voice what they want, while also giving you a chance to speak your mind! This may help you come across as less aggressive while still getting your point across at the same time.

This is not only brilliant advice when it comes to disagreeing with bosses, but in any situation where there are disagreements - whether personal or work related. Disagreement doesn't mean that everything becomes an argument; just be professional about how you go about voicing disagreement so that both parties know what's going on and clearly understand how things should be handled moving forward.

In order to avoid arguments in a disagreement, don't make assumptions before getting all the information first. Ask questions if something isn't clear and let them lead the conversation until everyone is on the same page.

The same goes for disagreeing respectfully when discussing a disagreement. Be clear about your point but also be able to look at the situation from their perspective and see how it could go wrong if they follow through with what you are suggesting. This will not only help them (and you) come up with better ideas but will make sure that no one is just going along blindly because they think this is easier than listening to other opinions or finding out more information before making any decisions.

It's also important to know that being professional doesn't mean agreeing either as well - there needs to be room in order to have disagreements and working together towards solutions without feeling like one person always has things completely figured out.

How to Stand Up Against an Unreasonable Boss

SOME BOSSES CAN BE downright unreasonable and condescending, but this doesn't mean you should take it lying down. Standing up to your boss is not as easy as it sounds. If you don't do it properly, then they can end up bullying you or driving you out of the company. However, there are ways you can stand up for yourself and even show them how unreasonable they are being.

Many people feel helpless when faced with a superior who is being stubborn, but there are ways for us to take control of the situation and handle it better. There are ways on how you can hold your ground against an unreasonable boss as well as how you can stand up to them and not let the bullying get to you.

The first step is to always try your best to avoid them as much as possible, or if you must speak with them, make sure not to let their words get under your skin. This is having the self-control of not reacting to their bully, and hopefully it will die off when they see that their silly act is not having any effect on you.

Another way to stand up for yourself against an unreasonable boss is by learning how to not be so sensitive, at least not to all the words they said. You need to learn what they are getting out of being stubborn with you and move past it. Learning this will help you remain calm in the face of their bullying tactics, which can make them feel like less powerful because you are not reacting to their words.

What you can also do is to lead them to engage in a meaningful conversation (especially if it's a sensitive topic) with them, but do not let it turn into an argument or debate as this can only lead to one person caving in and being put on the defensive. If you think that the conversation is leading to nowhere, then stop it and go back to your tasks. Hold the conversation off till the next better time.

In some situation, you can also confront them about their behavior, but you shouldn't do this in front of other people, as they will only make the situation worse. If you feel confrontation will lead to an unproductive argument for your side, or if the person criticizing you don't understand the point you're trying to make, it might be best to stay away from them because staying close with a person who does nothing but put you down is never healthy for your mental health.

Unreasonable bosses get their satisfaction from the feeling of power over others. Thus, it is important to not show fear or weakness in front of them so that they don't continue with this behavior and feel confident enough to bully other people as well. There may come a point where we need to give up on whatever project or goal that was set out because it's just too much work and time putting into something that isn't worth what we're getting. Learning how to best stand up against an unreasonable boss takes practice, patience, and luck!

Knowing When is the Perfect Time to Speak with Your Boss

IN YOUR WORKPLACE, IT is easy to get caught up in your daily tasks and forget that there are other people who you work with. It is important to have conversations regularly with those around you for several reasons, but it can be difficult when everything else seems more pressing than taking time out of your day. Knowing when to speak with your boss about something can be tricky because they are busy as well.

How do you know when the time is right to discuss a topic with your boss? This question may seem like a silly one, but it's not. I can confidently tell you that this is one of the most important factors to get your boss to agree to your request. Imagine when you were a child and wanted the toy so badly. How did you make your parent buy it for you? Did you ask when they are in good spirits or when they are in a foul mood? Now you see the point?

I know this might even feel stressful for some people out there. There are many factors that go into knowing whether now is the perfect opportunity to request a moment of their time. As I mentioned earlier, you wouldn't want to ask when your superior is in a foul mood, as they may not be in a good position to listen. You wouldn't want to bother them when they are busy with someone else's time either, such as actively brainstorming for an upcoming project or running errands.

If it were something personal that you want to talk about, then perhaps during their lunch hour might be best; but if you needed feedback on an idea that was due yesterday, maybe waiting until later tonight would be more appropriate so that there isn't any pressure about finishing up work at the end of today's meetings.

When you cannot request a private conversation with your superior, you may ask a colleague to help you with this. This provides the boss an opportunity to set up a mutually convenient time and is less daunting than other strategies such as using email or texting, although this may not be the best approach since your boss may totally forget about it or set a time later than you would have preferred.

Another factor to consider is to first ask yourself what you want to talk about. If it's something that can be discussed in a quick, casual manner, then there are probably other better times for this conversation. However, if you know your boss has been thinking about it too and they would like some time with you over lunch or coffee, then go ahead and start making plans for when will work best for both parties involved. The worst thing to do is wait until all their free time is taken up because then there might not be any right time at all!

To ensure that it is a meaningful conversation, it's good to give your boss an idea of how long your meeting will last so that they can plan accordingly. And if you can give a quick liner on what the meeting will be about allows everyone to know exactly where their focus should be.

When you're finally at the stage to set a time for the meeting, be specific. Instead of something vague like "when you're available" or "if you don't have plans" say, "Would Friday at 8:00 or 10:00 work?"

The more specific you are with your requested schedule, the better chance there is that your boss can set aside and plan for your requested meeting. Letting them know about the moment ahead of time (as opposed to surprising them), allows them enough planning and ensures nothing comes up in those moments where they might have had a different plan.

Build a Strong Relationship with Your Boss That Will Help You in the Future

BUILDING GOOD RAPPORT WITH your boss is key when starting a smooth dialogue! It will be easier to carry out any future tough conversations if you have good talking terms with your boss now. It's important to build a strong relationship with your boss right from day one so they will trust you and hear your opinion and take you seriously. They should also get to know you better as a person, so they'll be more likely to trust you because they understand your character and personality. I can't stress enough that it's so important for you to build a strong relationship with them!

A strong relationship with your boss is one of the greatest assets you can have in your workplace. Even if you don't have a magnificent work ethic, if your boss likes you enough, they'll likely give you more opportunities to improve, to hear your opinion and suggestions. And if they trust you and respect what you say, it's even easier for them to take risks on your behalf or help you out in other ways. The better their opinion of you, the more valuable an employee they will consider you to be. All this makes any future progression so much easier!

There are many ways to build a strong relationship with your boss. A few that worked well for me are being friendly and respectful, making them feel appreciated by thanking them often or volunteering by helping out when needed and never talking badly about their other employees in front of the boss! Whilst it may be too extreme to invite your boss over to dinner occasionally, and occasional homemade cookies and muffin for your boss can go a long way!

Another way is simply by being yourself. It's all too easy for people who are in positions of power, such as bosses, to see their employees through filters and expectations that don't reflect how they really are or what the person has contributed. If you can be open and honest about who you are, then it will make building a good professional relationship so much easier! Don't fall into the trap of putting a front and behave like a "model employee" in front of your boss. You do not want to portray yourself as a hypocrite by your coworker, and worse, by your boss.

After-work drinking sessions are another great way to bond with your boss. This is the time where everyone is not tense up and people loosen up after a few drinks. It's the perfect time to have a casual conversation with your boss. Things are less formal and it's easier to talk about anything.

Finding common interests like music, sport teams, hobbies may give you an insight into what makes them tick. When people share a common interest, it is easier to connect with them. Attending company social events can also provide a good chance to strengthen your relationship with your boss, but many people had often neglected this because they see it as "time wasting". They preferred to spend time with family to "wasting" time in those company events. I'm not saying this is wrong, but if you can find a balance between the two, you will benefit in the long term.

How to Make Your Boss Fall in Love with You

IF YOU ARE LIKE me, then this is a question that you will ask yourself every day. I have had bosses who loved me and others whom I am not sure they even know my name. My guess is they probably don't! I've always heard people say that one of the best feelings in life is to know that family and friends like you. But it can be quite challenging with making our boss like us.

We've all had that boss who doesn't seem to care about you as much as they should. You know the one - they don't really like your ideas, give you enough work for a full-time position, and often criticize you for no apparent reason at all. Not only is this frustrating, it also makes working in the office more difficult because you can never be sure if your boss likes or dislikes what you're doing.

So how do you deal with these types of bosses? It's tough to figure out how to get him on your side. If things turned out to be so bad, should you just quit your job and find another one? Of course not! There are ways to improve their opinion of you so that they love you (or at least like you), even if it takes some time and effort on your part.

Here are a few ideas to get started:

1. Show that you're highly committed. You can do this by working late or coming in early, taking on extra work outside of your job description, and doing anything else necessary for the sake of

your company's success. Some may disagree on this, particularly from those who value "work-life balance". But the fact is you cannot deny that this works! Of course, if you are in early for the morning coffee and newspaper and staying late in the office while binge watching YouTube, then you are just going to create more trouble for yourself. If you reach office early and leaving slightly later to rush off an important project, it shows that you are taking your work seriously, and know how to set prioritize your work. This usually go well with bosses.

2. Take charge. If there is something wrong with how things are typically done in the office (such as meeting times being too unproductively short or too inefficiently long), come up with a better solution and present it to everyone involved so everyone can all benefit from it.

3. Offer constructive criticism when someone does something wrong - not just pointing out what they did incorrectly but also showing them how they could have done things differently, so he doesn't make those same mistakes again. This is leadership quality and might help to set you up for promotion in the future.

4. Add value to the team. If you are asked to do something, offer suggestions on how it could be done more efficiently or with better quality - or get a new perspective by trying out the task yourself and reporting back what went well and what didn't work so much (and why). Share your experience and insights to improve the processes.

5. Show empathy. When your boss is going through some tough times outside of work, let him know you heard about it from someone else; he'll appreciate knowing that there's no need for him to recount all the bad things happening in his life when he already has enough stress at home. This can be personal and sensitive, so

unless you are in great talking term if your boss, it might not be appropriate to talk about it.

6. Be patient. We've all had bosses who don't seem especially nice at first, but as time goes on, and you get to know each other better, they start showing their wonderful qualities of a boss - so keep an open mind, be cool and wait for it.

7. Show appreciation and gratitude. Your boss is also a human being, and he deserves to know that you appreciate the work he does for the company - so make sure every once in a while, tell him how great the company is and how the latest product or processes has helped to make the company stronger, or made your work easier.

8. Be proactive with feedback. Sometimes it's difficult to get an honest evaluation of your own work from your boss who has to deal with its consequences daily; if this sounds like something that might happen in your office, then take matters into your own hands and give yourself some positive reinforcement. Feedback to your boss anything before it becomes a major issue. Your boss will take notice of you and appreciate your contribution. You are worth so much more than what you think of yourself, and others will see it too!

9. Do tasks outside of just the project assigned. Handle this well because you don't want to be seen as just a worker bee who blindly does any task assigned. Learn to pick the right tasks. If you know there's something that your boss really needs done but he hasn't asked for it, for example, if your boss is too busy and doesn't have time to delegate out those responsibilities, then offer what work may help him get ahead on the projects. Remember, this can also mean pitching an idea or two of your own! This initiative and thinking outside the box will reinforce your value within his department.

Don't Talk to Your Boss Like You're Talking to a Friend

THE WORST THING YOU can do when talking to your boss is to be talking to them like they are your friend. There has to be a basic respect for your boss, and you can't simply talk about anything under the sun. Your boss is not here to hear about how happy your dog makes you or what type of coffee you like best. Your boss is not your friend; they are the person who makes sure that you get paid and has the power to fire you if necessary.

If you are on the other extreme and you feel like it will bother your boss too much if you use formal language, there are other ways of being respectful without using an overly formal tone. For example, instead of saying "I would appreciate it if we could speak about this later," say something like "if I may ask" or "please."

I've labeled below a list of Dos & Don'ts to serve as a guidance to your conversation with your boss. It will help you have a proper conversation, to help you stay in line in your day to day dealing and conversation with them.

Dos:

1. Do be polite and respectful towards your boss. As much as you like to break the ice and build a powerful bond with them, they're the person who gives you work, so strive to balance a formal relationship with them.

2. Do make eye contact when you're talking to your boss: It's important that you do that because it shows that you're engaged in the conversation, and it also makes them feel comfortable because they know that you're paying attention to what they have to say.

3. Do speak up when you have a question, concern, or idea for improvement. You know what they say? If you don't speak up, people won't hear you. So if there's something that bothers you or something you want to change around here, just voice it out!

4. Do be honest with your boss about them. There's no two ways about it. Even if they aren't the most understanding person, you still have to put your foot down sometimes. You do not want the misunderstanding to go on forever and make things difficult in the future.

5. Do have a plan for how you want the conversation to go. Have a good idea of how the conversation with your boss should be and execute it well. There's no need to worry about anything, persevere and just be yourself, and never digress.

6. Do be honest with your boss about what you want to do. Honesty is always the best policy. Tell them about what you want to do and how you will do it, and then how they can help you achieve those goals.

7. Do learn more about your company's culture and values before you raise any concern to your boss. When you do, show that it aligns with them.

8. Do give feedback constructively. Don't just say "I hate this" or "These sucks": I found that giving constructive feedback to my boss has been really helpful. I used to be afraid of telling him things like he could do better, but some of the feedback it actually became a

good conversation starter and got the ball rolling on improving how we work together.

9. Do ask for help if needed. Sometimes we need help from our boss, and it's ok to ask. They're there for a reason. As long as your request is reasonable, they are likely to agree to your request. If you feel you needed extra help to complete your project on time, it is best to seek additional help and not delay the completion. I'm sure your boss will be more than willing to help you with that!

10. Do Keep an open mind about new ideas and feedback from your boss. When you're working for someone, the key thing to remember is that they know more than you. Be open-minded about new ideas and feedback from your boss. They may not be always right, but he might have some valuable feedback for you which you can improve on.

Don'ts

1. Don't interrupt your boss when they're talking. This is basic and in fact you shouldn't be interrupting anyone when they are talking. Besides being rude to your boss, it can also be a way of showing your disrespect for their position as well. You don't want to make them think that you're irresponsible, or worse, disrespectful.

2. Don't gossip about your coworkers or complain about them to your boss. Complaining to your boss and badmouthing coworkers is a waste of time; instead, focus on the positive aspects of working there.

3. Don't talk too much and let other people get a word in edgewise. People often talk too much and listen too little. You should be quiet sometimes and listen to others, especially towards your boss. The more you hear from them, the clearer ideas you will have about what they want, so you can better fit their expectation.

4. Don't lie to your boss. This is the worst thing you can do and don't even consider lying to them. You'll get found out one day or either that you will need more lies to cover up. And if you lie, they may just fire you for dishonesty.

5. Don't make assumptions about what your boss wants from you - always ask first. It's a good idea to know what your boss expects from you. It helps you make sure that their expectations align with yours, and it keeps the lines of communication open so that they're clear about what you are doing.

6. Don't blame other people for mistakes that were made by you or someone else in the company. We're all human and we make mistakes. Sometimes those mistakes were because of someone else's fault, or perhaps something beyond our control happened to us. Though that doesn't really matter.

7. Don't be afraid to make a legit request. For example, don't be afraid of asking for a raise if you deserve it. Not asking for a raise could be the biggest mistake of your career. The worst that can happen is they say no and you'll have the same salary as before.

8. Don't forget that your boss is also human, and they have feelings too. Your boss is just as human as you are and don't be afraid to show them you care about their well-being too.

9. Don't hesitate to voice out or raise a concern. Don't be afraid to speak out if you notice something that isn't right or if there's something that makes you feel uncomfortable. You could help the company by voicing it out early, before things get any worse.

10. Don't be late for work all the time. If you're a little late for work now and then, it's not too big of a deal. Just try to be on time most of the time. If you show up late to work all the time, your boss is going to get pretty fed up and if this happens enough, they'll

eventually fire you. Not much conversation can help. Even for us, we all hate that someone who is always late for work.

Concluding Part I

SO WE HAVE COME to the end of Part I in this book, which has been all about mastering the skills you need to be successful when talking with your boss. We also learned how to find the right moment to achieve our goals and why it is important not to neglect the soft skills when building a powerful bond with them.

In Part II, we will discuss tips on handling various challenging topics like how to handle a difficult conversation or giving feedback, especially when the issues on hand lie with the boss themselves. Sometimes there's no way to escape from this conversation, and discussions about sensitive issues are necessary in order for them to understand the problem at hand.

You will also learn how to handle a conversation if the problem is with you. When it comes to talking about your not so stellar performance, there are certain skills and phrases that can help represent what's going on in an incredibly authentic way.

I would suggest paying attention and learn more of the tips shared in part II because those tips I'm going to share will help you feel more confident and in control of the situation, especially when it is all seemed to be not in your favor. If you are skillful enough, they may well turn it in your favor!

Before you go to the next section, take sometimes to think through what you'd picked up in Part I. Write notes about your previous encounters and see how you might adopt what you learned in Part I in those scenarios. You should now be able to see how you could have handled it better. Have a mental roleplay, and practice how you should be reacting. Once you are all good, let's move on to Part II.

PART II

How to Handle Difficult Conversations with the Boss in Different Situations

THERE ARE MANY TOUGH conversations that you can have with your boss throughout your career, and these range from how to handle (bad) performance reviews, how to talk about compensation and or even how to ask for a promotion.

The more complicated ones come when it is not clear who the responsibility lies in, such as raising an issue or conflict that happened at work without implicating another person or asking for a pay raise if you think you truly deserve it.

The difficulties come in different degree depending on which is the problem: whether it comes from you, or your boss. How do you start a conversation when the fault lies on your boss?

In the following chapters, I will broadly categorize the various situations into four major sources of issues; issues lie on your boss, issues related to workplace, concerns related to career, and personal non work-related problems. These scenarios are so common that you will see them repeating over and over again throughout your career. At any point when you are facing a similar situation, you can always refer to this book to learn how to handle them.

Before we begin this chapter, first look at the few pointers that I'd listed below. Those are some good basic concepts that you can pick up in order to handle a tough conversation well.

1. Keep your cool in all situations. A discussion may or may not turn out well. Stay calm and don't argue back with them, even if you disagree with their point of view. If things are getting heated, take a break and come back later with fresh eyes to discuss it again.

2. Listen to what they're saying without getting defensive or angry. You may have raised your points, but also listen to what they have to say from their perspective. Sometimes we get caught up with our current situation but failed to see it from the corporate's perspective. Things may not be as easy as it seems, but the entire purpose of the conversation is to see how you and your boss can make it better. Therefore, it is always good to acknowledge the other person's feelings and be empathetic.

3. Try not to be too emotional about it. You can ask for what you want, but you may not get it. So learn to compromise. It is good to keep an open mind because you never know that the new suggested solution may actually be better than what you had in mind!

4. Finally, if all else fails, take a break. It is pointless to force a conversation if you think it is leading to nowhere. If you are in this situation, it is important to show that you do not accept the conclusion, but also accept the fact that the current moment is not conducive for a fruitful conversation. If the situation allows, respectfully ask for another session where you can discuss the issues in greater depth.

I have used these 4 tips with great successes, and I strongly advise you to adopt it. If used properly, you will see that they can help you hold an important discussion better. Many people lose the game when they get too emotional in a heated conversation and later find it difficult to come back for another round of discussion. But if you followed the pointers closely, it should not happen to you.

With these tips in mind, let's move on to look at how to handle each difficult conversation with your boss.

When the Problem lies with Your Boss

How to Talk to Your Boss About His Behavior That Displeases You

ONE MIGHT NEVER EXPECT a bad day on the job from time to time, but there are many instances where employees find themselves unhappy in their position due solely to whom they report over - their manager being just one example. In fact, this is one of the most common sources of workplace stress when one has an unsatisfactory relationship with the boss.

But what happens if these frustrations turn into consistent dissatisfaction? If this has been affecting you and you don't address your concerns to them directly, it can really affect both your work and personal life.

Unless you're able to find a new job that pays just as well, your best bet is probably telling them about the problems. While it's okay to approach your boss about issues that bother you; however, everything has its place when speaking up!

Boss management is a delicate process, and how to talk about behavior that displeases you can be difficult. The first thing you need to remember is that the two of you have different perspectives on the situation. Your perspective as an employee could differ completely from their perspective as a business owner or management role. The first step is to think about how their perspective might differ from your own. He could have a completely different outlook on the situation that led him to take this action, even if he had no ill intentions. It's important at this point for you to recognize when their motivations are genuine and not just out of spiteful behavior. Once you can see past these motives, then address your complaints appropriately!

You also need to make sure that the two of you are talking about it from the same angle before coming up with solutions together. You may find yourself repeating things over again because they don't understand what exactly needs fixed; however, by being willing and open-minded enough, differences can be resolved.

Another great diplomatic way is to look for the opportune moment to provide an honest constructive feedback to your boss. This is also one of the best ways to help them improve. Unless his attitude and behavior are specifically directed towards you, then chances are that others will feel the same way about him. It can be difficult for bosses to realize that certain behaviors annoy everyone. But it's also understandable how they might not even notice! Without truthful feedback, it's likely that their performance (or the entire organization's) will suffer, and they'll continue making the same mistakes without knowing. Telling your boss about your dissatisfaction will help them find alternative ways to improve abilities by identifying their blind spots through constructive feedback. From the positive point of view, if everyone in your department does this regularly, it could really help the entire department.

A good point to take note is that in order to discuss your boss' behavior when you are dissatisfied by their actions, it's best to wait until they ask for input directly, or indirectly. You do not want to appear as disrespecting his or her authority. And when they ask for feedback, give them feedback respectfully.

On some occasion, negative working relationships are not within the realm of possibility to resolve and might work best with seeking help in elsewhere, such as with the Human Resources department. Even the most successful organizations are not immune to conflicts and disagreements. There may be moments where third-party intervention is necessary to help resolve a dispute or disagreement among colleagues. Personally, I will attempt that at the last resort.

Another good subtle way of approaching it is using the "see it, follow it." approach. For example, I used to have a direct manager who often "skip lunch" and will do a quick bite in the office, munching away sandwiches while she works. She always leaves an hour earlier from the usual knock off hour each time she does that. That continued until one fine day, I enquired if I could do the same, but I got denied. But since then, she stopped doing that too!

Now if you observe a troublesome behavior consistently, you can always try to inquire about company flexibility and suggest to the department that you may want to follow suit. This will usually set a kind of feedback to their action, and if indeed the organisation is moving towards that direction, then the animosity will diffuse, and everybody is happy.

How to Talk to Your Boss When They are Wrong

WE ALL HAVE THOSE moments when we disagree with our boss. You know that feeling when you have to tell your boss they're wrong? It's terrifying. We might not talk about it, but what do you do when your disagreement is still on your mind?

It's tough to know how to approach a situation like this without upsetting your boss or risk getting fired for insubordination. But before you give up and let the awkwardness fester, you can try out some ways that can help make the conversation easier. Start with any of these 3 openers that are less intrusive.

1. "Hey, boss! I noticed you could have made a mistake." This is an excellent strategy when you want to bring attention to something without being too direct. It's also helpful if your boss usually responds defensively or dismissively, which they might do because of their ego. By cushioning your statement with "could have", it set a stage that allows them to take responsibility without feeling attacked or defensive.

2. "Boss, could we chat about this?" This opener will give you a chance to sit down with your boss and talk through the issue without it coming across as an attack or confrontation. This is an excellent strategy if you want to have an open dialogue without seeming confrontational. When using this phrase, make sure that when delivering it, your tone conveys the seriousness of the

situation — you don't want them to think it's just something insignificant.

3. "I'm sorry if I'm being too forward, but I think there's an issue here." This is the most direct approach, and this is also the best strategy to use when you think your boss doesn't realize there's a problem. When using this statement, make sure that you're polite but firm in how confident you sound — you want to show them how serious the matter is without seeming pushy or overbearing.

How to Talk to Your Boss About a Problem that Lies with Him

NOBODY IS PERFECT, NEITHER is your boss. How do you talk to your boss about a problem that they might not know they have? This is a question many employees ask themselves when they are trying to figure out how to handle the situation. Before you even attempt to raise it to them, you'll need to first understand how your boss might react if they are unaware of their problem or unacceptable behavior.

Some bosses will be open and receptive when faced with a problem that has been brought forth by an employee. They may take responsibility for the situation and ask what they can do to fix it. Other bosses may become defensive or attack the person, bringing up the issue from not understanding it properly because they don't want to take responsibility for their actions. The best way to handle this is calmly explain why there's a problem so that he understands without making them feel attacked (i.e., "I'm trying to work on X project, but I keep running into roadblocks because _____").

I'll share more ways on how you can approach this complicated issue:

1. Do not bring up the problem right away. Instead, start with a positive comment about how you are thrilled working at your organization or how much you enjoy their projects so far. This will

put them in a more receptive mood for what is coming next. This is a great way to start, because you are making the other party feel good and you are opening the topic on a positive note.

2. Ask questions that can lead to your topic, even if they don't mention it themselves. These could be as simple as "What do you think of my work?" and "How did things go this week?". If they still haven't brought it up, you can continue and lead to the topic by saying something like "I think there might be a problem. I've been feeling the need to talk with you for some time."

3. Talk about how this issue is affecting your work life or your ability to do good in their company and that they have yet to make any comments or feedback on how things are going (An example of opener: "I feel like my performance has slipped because of these problems"). This is a wonderful opportunity to talk about the problem, and you can frame it in such a way that your boss can be part of the solution. This is a perfect resolution because effectively, you are making him to be part of the solution to solve the issues, rather than accusing him to be the problem of the fault.

4. Raise the issue but show them you're willing to help fix the problem by coming up with solutions together. This could include making lists of what's working well now and what needs improvement or brainstorming ideas together before implementing one at a time until everything improves accordingly. This technique is not about pinpointing whose fault it is, although usually the raising of problems would have clearly shown who caused the problem.

5. Be polite and ask whether something has been difficult for them lately because it might affect the performance of the projects (e.g., deadlines have slipped). You want to frame it in such a way

that you are not accusing them of anything. Be careful when executing this technique because, as we mentioned earlier, some bosses will not be receptive to this.

If none of this works, then it's time for a more serious conversation about whether there is an underlying problem and what steps need to be taken to fix it. You want to frame this as not being personal but "fixing" a work relationship together, which will benefit both parties.

How Do You Tell Your Boss That They're a Bad Communicator

TELLING YOUR BOSS THAT they are a poor communicator is rarely something you want to do. They might take it personally because they don't like being told anything's wrong with them. That doesn't mean there isn't an issue though! Poor communication can often lead to projects going off-course without notice or missing important details necessary to achieving their goal.

There will be times when this happens no matter how good at communicating someone may be, but if it happens more than half of the time, then odds are yes, your boss needs some help in articulating better. It's not your place to tell them they're a poor communicator, but it is possible to hint at the issue without being too direct.

The first step would be to assess what type of things are going wrong and how often this happens. If there are minor problems every once in a while, then you have nothing to worry about! However, if errors seem common and happen more than half the time, then it could mean that their style of communicating isn't working for everyone involved.

There are some techniques that you can use to help the boss improve on expressing certain ideas. For example, if they are trying to explain something and you notice that they have a tough time conveying the idea and message, you can ask them, "Could you please repeat what I just heard?" That will allow them to take more time in articulating their thoughts. This will also give you a chance to take notes and perhaps ask more questions.

If they are giving out important information, then it is best if you could summarize the key points for them before proceeding with your work. This will ensure that there won't be any confusion or miscommunication when going over these details with other colleagues later on.

You can also remind them about how the people at their level feel by saying "I think this is an idea worth considering" during meetings. This way they'll know that someone has been listening and acknowledging to what they'd said so far, and this will make them feel they should be careful to not misrepresent any information.

Finally, when you feel that the information provided doesn't add up or suspect that there is some key information that is missing, you can ask questions like, "how do we know this?" or "why did it happen?". Asking those types of open-ended questions often leads the boss into explaining some finer points which they may had missed from their original explanation.

In all essence, when giving feedback about how your boss communicates, try not to sound too passive aggressive as there's always a chance that they don't realize how bad at communicating they really are! Remember to always do it tactfully and respectfully because it's a sensitive subject to talk about for all parties involved.

How Do You Confront a Trash Talking Boss

I HOPE THIS NEVER happens to you because it will be really disheartening to be in an office where the boss is trash talking about you. If it happens, will you know how to deal with your boss?

I know how hard it can be to hear about your boss talking trash behind your back, but it is important that you hear directly from them and not through other people. The best way is to confront them and ask for constructive feedback. This can be difficult, but it will help you emotionally and improve your performance in the long run. As an employee, you want to hear from your boss when they are not happy with how you're performing. You deserve the opportunity to fix things and make changes that will improve your performance.

Some employees may feel afraid of getting fired or not meeting expectations if they bring up their concerns. But thing will get worse if you don't address it soon. The good news is that there are other simpler approaches you can try to talk to your boss before resorting to awkward confrontation.

You can first try speaking to your boss about what you had heard and verify with them. The important thing here is to make sure you have the right information. For example, your boss may not be aware of how and what other people are talking to you, and it would need better understanding on their part before correcting them or asking others to stop. This also provides the perfect chance to clarify any misunderstanding, or to realign any expectation.

If you can confirm or if your boss admitted trash talking about you, then you may confront them to stop it. You can also choose not to work for this person anymore if it is too difficult or if it gets too uncomfortable. But if your primary goal is to resolve the issues, it's important to frame this situation relating to how it is affecting you and the company culture, highlighting that the consequences are not just yourself. The goal should always be to restore lines of communication so both parties can work things out together when there are problems. Be prepared that you may continue to be criticized by your boss but hold firm that you have the interest of the organization at heart.

If your boss claims not to know anything about what you're talking about, maintain your ground and deliver whatever needs to be said. This way, if they had indeed trashed-talk about you, they'll be less likely to do it again since they know word has gotten back to you. If not, then maybe this will help prevent this from happening in the future.

It Can Be Tricky to Handle Workplace Related Topic

How to Talk to Your Boss About Toxic Co-workers

MANY OF US HAVE had to deal with a toxic co-worker at some point in our careers. In the past, I used to just avoid them and hope they would go away. But I realized I can't do it all the time. One of the hardest parts about dealing with a toxic co-worker is trying to figure out why they're being so mean. Whether it is an aggressive personality or someone who spreads rumors about you, dealing with these types of co-workers can be difficult and stressful. This can feel frustrating and pointless. If it's happening to you, it's important that you take some action and talk to your boss before things get anything worse. Here's what you can do:

1. Schedule a meeting with your boss. Approach your boss and ask if they have any free time to chat. They will most likely say yes, and you can then discuss your concerns with them. In this meeting, let's pretend that your boss is named Steve. You should start by telling him about the things that make the coworker toxic: "Steve, I wanted to talk to you about my coworker Jane because she has been pretty difficult lately."

You may have a list of specific incidents in mind - for example, maybe they are spreading rumors or yelling at other people. One thing you don't want to do is focus on their personality type alone; there could be many reasons behind why someone might act like this. So try not to generalize too much right off the bat since it doesn't help anybody solve anything.

2. Ask your boss what the company's policy is for handling toxic co-workers. Explain that you'd like to talk about one of your coworkers, but don't give away too many details. If you don't feel comfortable telling your boss about the incidents, then just tell them that this person has been difficult to work with lately. The more specific problems you mention though, the easier it will be for your boss to help. If they ask what you would like from them on a personal level, let them know all you want is an apology or some time away from this person. You can also have a coworker accompany you if one of those options doesn't sound appealing.

Not every company's policy is going to look exactly alike so there may not be any blanket guidelines, but whatever happens make sure that nothing else escalates and try not get carried in order to avoid unnecessary drama at work; keep calm and focus on solving the immediate problem.

3. Be prepared to explain the situation and provide examples of how the coworker is toxic. For example: The coworker is constantly making fun of you, He is always talking about how stupid your ideas are and they even criticize how you do work sometimes, etc.

4. Record the incidents and share this information with your boss discreetly so that they can take action. Ask how they would handle the situation, or what advice they might have for you but be ready for your boss's response, which may include asking you to deal with it yourself or telling you they'll talk to them directly.

HOW TO TALK TO YOUR BOSS WHEN YOU ARE UNHAPPY AT WORK

DO YOU DREAD GOING to work every day? Does it feel like your best days are behind you? You're not alone. Recently, I had an interesting chat with one of my mentees. She said that she was unhappy at work and wanted to know how to talk to her boss about it. It sounded like she has been enduring all the unhappiness, and I know this is a common problem for many people because she wasn't the only one asking me for advice on how they can address the issue.

The truth is, many employees find themselves in the same boat - unhappy at work and unsure how to fix it. But the way to solve this problem is really very simple; If you are not happy at work, then raise it up to your boss as soon as possible. It's important that you don't ignore these feelings for too long; ignoring them can lead to bigger problems down the line.

From my conversations with many of these people, many find it hard to talk to their boss about being unhappy at work because they fear like they are risking your job, or that the problem is not big enough for him to take action. If you feel the same, then I have to advise that you shouldn't. Look at it this way, negative vibes, work stress, unhappiness all affect business productivity. The boss will more than likely to help you address your concerns because this will benefit both the organization and yourself in the long run.

Therefore, it's important to have an open and honest conversation with your boss early on so they know how you're feeling and what steps they need to take in order to address any issues you have. There are a few simple ways of how you can speak with your boss about this.

The first way to have an open and honest conversation with your boss is by being direct. This may seem like a daunting task, but it's necessary for him to know how you're feeling so that he can address any issues you have at work. You should prepare and go into the discussion knowing what exactly it is about, whether it's about something specific or just general unhappiness in the workplace.

If there are certain occurrences that make you feel unhappy daily, then try using this technique: when these events happen, note them and mention each one during your meeting with your boss so they're aware of all the problems going on around you.

Sometimes, the unhappiness could be because of a lack of growth within the organization. If this is the case for you, then try mentioning your aspirations to be promoted or take on additional responsibility so you can feel fulfilled and satisfied in your work. If you have problems at home or a family crisis, then you'll need to decide whether to share any personal details. Let your boss know you need to take time away from work and address the issue at home if necessary. Your boss would more likely agree to an arrangement with so that you can focus on what is necessary before returning to work.

I have put together guided steps to help you with your preparation and thought process:

1. Find out what is making you unhappy.
2. Figure out whether it's something that you can change.

3. If the problem is with your boss, talk to them about it. Consider your boss's perspective. Talk to your boss about why you're unhappy and how they can help.

4. If the problem isn't with your boss, talk to HR about it.

5. Be honest and don't hold back - if you're upset, they need to know.

6. Don't let this affect how well you do at work in other areas of responsibility.

7. Put together a plan for how you will address these problems, so they don't happen again.

8. If the problem is more than just a disagreement, consider whether it might be time for a change in jobs.

How to Talk to Your Boss That You are Overworked or Just Too Busy

IT'S DIFFICULT TO TALK to your boss when you think you're overworked, but it's something that needs to be done. If you don't speak up, no one will know how much work is on your plate and the pressure will continue to pile until it eventually gets unbearable.

There is no shame in being overwhelmed at work. In fact, many bosses won't realize you're overworked until you voice your concerns. If your plate is overflowing, you need to speak up to get things to change. No one wants to come across as lazy, uncommitted, or not a team player. But at the same time, it's important for you to know that if you don't change things up, then you're going to burn out and quit. So what can you do to strike a balance?

1. Speak up. Letting things fester only makes them worse. It's time to speak up about what is on your plate before it becomes unbearable. You don't have to tell him everything that bothers you; sometimes the simpler solution is better for both of you in the long run (e.g., "I'm feeling really stressed out from my workload right now", "The amount of work is overwhelming me and I'm feeling like it's affecting my productivity and quality at work."). Other times, though, they need all the details if there are specific issues that need solving. Be honest with yourself when deciding how much information is necessary to share.

2. Explain that you're doing everything in your power not to let this become a pattern and give examples of things you've already done, for example, cut back hours at home and started going into the office earlier so you could focus more time there during your business day.

3. If you feel like it's still too much for one person to handle, offer ideas of how they might distribute the load better - potentially by hiring someone new or request for a part-time intern. Your boss is usually aware of the number and type of employees they have on their payroll, so it will be up to you to express that there's an issue.

4. If you're not the only one feeling this way, mention that some of your coworkers have also expressed an interest in hiring a new person or requesting for more help. This will show management that you're serious about the problem, and it's not just you are being lazy.

5. Re-evaluate some of the routine tasks that can be a time sucker for you. If your job is to update a spreadsheet daily, for example, maybe let someone else do it every other day so that the time spent on this task doesn't add up across the week. Suggest the possibilities of delegating one part of your workload each day and check back in with that coworker to see how things are going if possible.

6. If your boss assigns you another project (on top of what you are already busy with), ask about the priority of this task so it doesn't impede on other projects. You can also point out what you are already working on to show that the newly assigned additional task ahead is not workable. This will also show him you are overworked and are likely to assign a more urgent project to another colleague.

How to Talk to Your Boss About Shifting Responsibilities

IT'S HARD TO TALK to your boss about something that you know will be a big change for them, and it can feel like an impossible conversation to have. But even if you don't want to leave your current position at work, there may come a time when you need or want to transfer internally.

Many employees are unhappy with their current position at work for many reasons. Maybe they have lost interest in the work, or maybe it is time to do something new and different. Whatever the reason might be, a job transfer can seem like a logical step to take next.

How do you go about asking your boss for an internal job change? In the past, this was a simple task. You would simply tell your boss that you wanted to move to another department, and they would either say yes or no. However, in today's world of competitive companies and employees vying for positions across departments, it is much more difficult to get such a request approved. In addition, organizations or departments will want to keep their most valued employees because it's expensive to train someone new; it costs a lot of time and work. This also means that it would be more sensible for the organization to have an established employee like you who can continue contributing. In some situations, your new potential boss might even be friends with your current one; as well as compete directly with them on projects. That is why it is particularly challenging to have these conversations without arousing any suspicion or triggering animosity from anyone involved.

There are a few steps you can follow in order to achieve your goal of moving departments. If you get it right, you might get your wish and move to the department or role of your choice. To talk to your boss about the changes, try out these few tips:

1. Find a moment when they are not too busy and best if they are also in good spirits. If you're lucky, this will be before or after productive meetings. The first thing you want to do is ask them what their thoughts are on the idea of you transferring departments, or even leaving entirely for another company. This will allow you to gauge how they feel about such an issue before asking them anything further. This also allows them some time to think more thoroughly about the option without feeling pressured by questions from you.

2. Plan for an informal chat where you can come to them confidentially around any concerns that might arise through transferring departments. In your private conversation, discuss sound options together and agree on mutually beneficial arrangements if possible. Be honest, but diplomatic. Share with them why you feel it's necessary to change your position and be open with them about any challenges you may face while making the transfer.

3. Spend some time researching who might be a suitable candidate to take over your duties if you depart. This could help make it easier for your boss to approve of the job change request since they will feel more confident with someone they already know taking this extra responsibility.

4. Be ready for objections from your boss if you are in a high-profile position. Your boss will most likely consider about the disruption to the current department before agreeing to your request. Think through what strategic concern your boss might have and prepare to suggest any solution. For example, consider if there's any suitable person you can recommend for promotion to assume your role? Can you train someone now to make sure there is minimal disruption? If you can discuss this transfer to another department professionally, it might just be easier to convince your boss.

However, if you're certain that your boss won't be receptive to the idea of a transfer, it's best not to dwell on the conversation too much. There are plenty of other opportunities out there and staying on in your current job provides some important skills and experience for a future career in another company.

HOW TO TALK TO YOUR BOSS WHEN YOU MESSED UP

IT'S AN UNFORTUNATE REALITY that it's often difficult to stay on top of everything at work. Working in a professional environment, there will be times when you mess up. Maybe you made an error on a project that could jeopardize the company's success or sent out sensitive information by accident. Anything can happen if you are not careful.

We all make mistakes, and the more open and honest you are about the matter, the better chance you have of resolving it quickly without getting into major trouble with your boss, or worse, fired from the job. The worst thing you can do is avoid talking about it and hope they don't notice. Follow these few tips to make it easier for you to talk to your boss about a work mistake:

1. Before you have the conversation with your boss, make a list of all potential damages. The more in-depth you are, the higher chance you have on damage control and preventing any future problems. Don't be afraid to take responsibility for your actions if it was a mistake on your part and apologize sincerely since trust is essential when working with someone.

2. Be direct and to the point. Take responsibility for the error. No matter what, an initial admission of guilt is necessary in order to have any chance at salvaging the situation with your boss. You don't

want them thinking that this could happen again or worse, think it's somehow their fault.

3. Explain how you're planning on fixing the problem and prevent it from happening again. Even if they feel angry or disappointed by what happened, most bosses will be open to hearing how you plan on correcting it so that it doesn't happen again.

4. If it's something that you can't fix right immediately, then explain what steps are being taken now to improve and prevent future occurrences from happening. This is also a good time to discuss new policies or procedures, so everyone knows how much they're expected to cooperate with each other in order for everything to go smoothly again.

5. Be polite and respectful. You don't want to come across as defensive or cocky, even if you're not entirely at fault for what happened. In the end it's your boss's decision how they'll react, so prepare ahead of time with a few responses in case things get heated.

To conclude, it's difficult to communicate with your boss, especially when you caused the mistake, but it is essential for trust and longevity at work. Be direct about what happened, how you plan on fixing it going forward, and ask for their input as well! You'll hopefully end up rebuilding some bridges while feeling better knowing that someone was listening to you, and seeing you taking ownership of the situation rather than letting it fester into something more serious down the line.

How to Talk to Your Boss and Convince Them to Let You Work Remotely

THE IDEA OF GOING to work every day can be daunting. Waking up early each day, get in your car and drive for 30 minutes to an hour each way, sit at a desk all day long, then go home and do it all over again tomorrow. If you're lucky enough not to live too far from your office but are still tired of the daily grind this commute is causing you, there's good news! There are plenty of companies out there that allow their staff to work from home. Sometimes you just have to ask for it!

Working from home is a great way to save time, money and sanity. But convincing your boss to let you work remotely can be an uphill battle. A common problem many remote workers have is that their boss doesn't want them working remotely because they think they will slack off or not be as good and productive at the job when there is no one to supervise you. They'll think that working from home means you'll do less work! But if you're lucky, your boss will find the idea of remote work appealing because it's cheaper than hiring someone full-time or paying for expensive office space in a major city. So how do you convince your boss and change their mind?

If you like the idea of trying to work from home and is thinking of speaking to your boss about it, perhaps the first thing you can do is your homework, and access if your company has the infrastructure and support in place to allow employee to work remotely. Back up your proposal with ideas and solution to the potential problem they may have. You can then suggest to your boss and share about how you can set up a system that will allow for transparency and accountability, so they'll know everything that's going on at all times.

May you can also suggest some "trial run" to your boss so they can access the feasibility of remote work. You may probably start with just one day in a week, or a fortnight, to see how things work out. If things continue to function seamlessly, then there will be a higher chance that remote working arrangement can materialize.

In order to persuade your boss to let you work from home, you must first establish your case that shows that they can trust your work ethic. For example, show that your work will be on the level, and you'll still put in the same amount of hours as an office worker. Put up a really compelling case, and if possible, also show how working remotely will help to improve the company's bottom line, where the saved commuting hours can mean more work being done.

Finally, if working from home is really non-negotiable for you, and you really need to work from home for a day or two, you can consider making an offer to make a financial sacrifice if that makes it more possible for them to consider allowing you to work remotely. You can suggest something like "I am okay with taking a pay cut for one year so long as I get to do my job from home." This type of offer may sound too good to pass up!

CAREER RELATED TOPICS

How to Talk to Your Boss When You're Underperforming

YOU HAVE A PERFORMANCE review coming up, and you're not sure how to prepare. You know your boss is going to ask you about the past six months and what you've been doing since then. What if it's nothing significant? That conversation will be awkward, but it can't hurt as much as when they ask how your performance has been. I have been in this similar situation twice in my career, and the second one really put me through countless sleepless nights. The company then was in an awful shape, and there was hearsay that they might lay employees off. I was new to the company, and my semi-annual sales target hadn't been quite on mark. So you can imagine how I felt back then.

I'm sure many employees have problems with their performance at work once in a while. They might be unsure of how to complete tasks, or they may lack motivation. If this also happens to you, what I will confidently advise you now is that it is important that you talk to their boss immediately about it so that you can resolve this problem sooner rather than later.

I know it can be extremely difficult to talk to your boss when you're underperforming because I'd been through that. But if you want to get back on track, it's necessary. It can frustrate when we don't know how to inform our boss and get back on track. But there are ways you can approach this conversation with your boss without appearing too needy or demanding.

These 4 tips will help you start a conversation with your boss and make sure you're on top of things again.

1. Try to stay composed in order to focus on the task at hand. Breathe deeply before talking to your boss about the problems you are experiencing at work. Don't panic, especially if you've had these issues in the past. It's not a life-or-death situation!

2. Be specific about what you communicate to your boss when discussing your work underperformance. When talking about how you're feeling and how it might affect your work, try not to generalize statements like "I'm struggling." Instead, say something more concrete and direct such as "I've been having a hard time following through with the tasks I need completed" or "I feel overwhelmed by my workload." This will give them better insight into where your problems are stemming from, and they may help solve your problem.

3. Acknowledge your underperformance without them raising it and suggest how you can improve the situation and communicate these during your meeting. This shows that you are taking ownership and responsibility for the subpar performance. The more you can offer as solutions, the better.

4. When communicating with your boss about performance review, also make sure that you are straightforward and honest. Do not make all excuses to cover up your weak job performance. Even if you are not 100% sure of all the reasons you're underperforming, make it a point to communicate this uncertainty with them anyway and ask what they would like you do moving forward.

It is key that you be open-minded during reviews so that your boss can help find solutions to your problems or issues at hand and work towards getting you back on track again. The goal when talking about performance review should be how to improve in the future rather than dwelling too much on past errors. Being honest about where things might have gone wrong will give your boss insight into how best to get things going right for you again! Just remember that underperformance isn't the same as lacking skill. Sometimes, it is because of circumstances outside your control - such as stress, illness or other life events, and more often than not, this is one-off.

How to Talk to Your Boss About Burnout

BURNOUT IS A COMMON state of mental and emotional exhaustion. It can happen to anyone who works hard, whether you work at home or in the office. Being burned out at work is a common experience that many people are familiar with. It's difficult to know how to address it, and even more difficult if you don't have any vacation time left. You can be as helpless as you can be.

There are a lot of reasons for people to burnout at work, including working remotely, working too many hours and juggling family needs. Regardless of how your burnout started though, there are steps you can take to help yourself recover and get back on track with your life and career. Usually, the simplest way is to ask your boss for a couple of hours of earlier release for the day, or day off for the long weekend. It's never a simple conversation to have with your boss though, albeit an important thing that you should do. If you're feeling burned out and your productivity has taken a hit because of it, then chances are you might not be the only one in the office who feels this way. As difficult as it may be to get up the nerve to talk about how exhausted you feel, there are ways that can help make this conversation easier for both parties involved.

1. It can be rather awkward, but you can start by telling your boss that you love the company, and you want to continue working with them before you highlight your concern and stating your request.

After all, if they don't know how important this is to you before the conversation starts, your boss may not believe that taking time off will benefit you and their business. It's also a good idea to mention that while burnout isn't contagious, you don't want to affect others in the office who feel similarly overworked.

2. Explain how you're feeling burned out and why it's making it hard to do your job. The more you can talk to your boss about the symptoms of burnout, how long they've been apparent, and how this has affected your work performance so far (this will help them understand why it's important for you to take time off), the better. Sometimes, your feelings might be a sign that something else may be happening in your life and is causing stress or anxiety. This could include personal issues like divorce or death; financial hardship; family problems; bullying at workplace; harassment on social media sites like Facebook or Twitter. Depending on the seriousness, your boss may even offer some other solutions other than just some day off.

3. Make sure not to sound too desperate when talking about this issue - don't use phrases like "I need help" or "I'm really struggling" because these phrases may imply that the problem is worse than it actually is, which could lead them to think that they have no choice but to displace you or put you on sabbatical leave, even if this isn't true. Instead, try using phrases like "I want my work here at ABC Company to be fulfilling again." or "I'm feeling really burned out lately because I've been putting all my energy into work with no time left for myself." Or "I find myself emotionally drained by my workload more often than usual these days."

4. Suggest ways for them to help - can they give you more time off, or a flexible schedule? Or would you be able to work from home

more often? It's important for them to hear your solutions and understand from you about what will help you revitalize your energy. What you propose may be a better solution because you know best how you work best.

5. If all else fails, ask for their advice on what other jobs might be suitable for someone with burnout. Is there any other role available? Is it possible to have a temporary placement where you can break away from a certain momentum to re-energize yourself?

How to Talk to Your Boss When You Feel Undervalued at Work

IT'S NO SECRET THAT people feel happier and more fulfilled at work when they're appreciated. When you don't get the recognition you deserve, it can affect your happiness and your job performance. One of the toughest parts of working in a big company is to speak up when you feel undervalued or overlooked. If you don't get enough due recognition for your excellent performance and significant contribution to your company, you will not get your promotion and pay raise. How do you overcome this and talk to your boss about it?

In the earlier part of my career, I didn't think that it was possible to create awareness and shout out to the entire world about my outstanding performances. I was lucky that it didn't take me long enough to understand that it can be done and how useful and important that it'd been for my steady career progression!

You may feel that your boss hasn't given you the recognition you deserve, but it's hard to know how to approach them and tactfully discuss the issue with them. Talking about these feelings can be difficult, but it's important to address them early so they don't get out of hand. Recognition is an excellent motivator for you, but if you do not correct it early on, it will have negative effects upon your morale and force you to consider jobs elsewhere. This may not be the most ideal outcome because you could miss out on great opportunities within the company. Moving to another company is hard as well. It takes a lot of time and effort to rebuild everything you had at your old job, which means it's even worse when all your efforts are in vain because the new employer may take more time to assess your capabilities.

What I want to assure you is that the conversation may not be as difficult as you think. Prepare well ahead and have your point set out clearly beforehand so you can articulate everything coherently. I've compiled a list of helpful tips on how you should go about having this conversation with your boss, so you get the best chance of receiving positive feedback from them!

1. Plan what you want to say. One way of feeling in control is having a crystal clear idea of how the conversation will go beforehand. Planning can help with this because it forces you to think about your feelings and articulate them clearer before going into the meeting. It also allows you to have laser-focused conversation on the matter at hand and not be thrown off by any distractions your boss might bring up.

2. Brainstorm together with a friend who has similar experiences. You can also write it down, organizing your thoughts in an orderly manner that makes sense as you go through them so when you speak about how undervalued you feel, they will understand where things are coming from without feeling judged or belittled for their position on the issue.

3. Know your worth. Before you talk to your boss, think about how much value you bring to the company. Write all your skills and accomplishments that have contributed positively to the company's bottom line. Know what is negotiable in your contract or job description before you get to any negotiation with your boss. This

will help you know ahead of time which things are worth discussing with them about feeling undervalued at work, so it won't be a surprise when they ask why this topic came up during the meeting.

4. Prepare some questions for them beforehand as well. If there's a problem that has been bothering you but hasn't gone away even after bringing it up earlier, prepare these questions beforehand so they can address those issues too.

5. Be prepared to negotiate. Your boss may or may not agree with the things you have to say, and that will affect what they offer in return. Your bargaining chips is how well you have helped the company in the past years. What you'll ultimately get depends on how well you put your case forward. Be confident in your abilities and what you've done for this company. It's all that really matters when talking about making a deal of any kind.

6. Ask for feedback and don't be afraid to ask questions about how you can grow within the company. Your boss may offer you another role to take on more responsibilities, so keep an open mind for new opportunities, even if they don't seem like a good fit at first glance. If you don't think there's anything that you can do about the situation, ask for more responsibility or a raise anyway. Sometimes it is really just a case of "ask and you shall be given."

7. Keep your cool because getting angry won't help anything. You can't fully predict how the boss will react to your conversation, so you have to remind yourself that it's just business and nothing personal. Don't be afraid to leave if things don't seem like they're going well. Sometimes it's just not worth fighting for something that will not change.

In summary, no one wants to feel undervalued, but when it happens, there are always many ways you can take the situation into your own hands and get what you want. It's not easy to ask for more recognition at work, but it can be worth the risk. Whether that means talking to your boss about how you're feeling or asking for more recognition at work in different forms such as a promotion or raise, or simply looking elsewhere if things don't turn out well, just be prepared and go with it.

How to Talk to Your Boss About Career Growth

AS A MILLENNIAL, YOU may wonder how to talk to your boss about career growth. Many millennials are looking for more responsibilities and opportunities that will help them grow in their careers. They also want feedback on how they're doing at work so they can well.

Career growth is a topic that every employee, no matter how senior you are in the role, should think about. But trying to talk to your boss about career growth can be a daunting task, especially when you are trying to navigate how you want your career to progress in a certain direction. How can you find the right way to talk about career growth with your boss? It's important to start by identifying what type of role you are looking for in order to figure out how best to approach this conversation. The right approach to this conversation can make all the difference, setting the stage for future career development and progression. Once you have a better idea, these next steps will help make the process go smoothly. It is simple, yet critical in achieving success.

1. Start by identifying areas of your career that you would like to grow in (for example, career goals, skills acquisition, etc.) This is where the semi-annual goal conversation comes into play. Make sure you have a schedule plan and are always on track with how these meeting sessions are going, so there's never any disconnect. Make

sure these conversations happen regularly as well for feedback sessions and support throughout your career journey with the company.

2. The next step is then asking your boss about what resources may be available at work, such as training workshops or company programs which can help achieve those identified growth points. This will clearly show your desire for a better performance and career growth. It will put you in pleasant light with your boss because you're not only showing how you want to grow but also show a willingness to help and improve yourself.

3. Be open and honest with your boss about what rank, job roles, or different company culture may be of interest for the next phase in your career journey. This will set a direction and provide an opportunity for them to have some input on how they can help you get there so that it's a win-win situation both ways. Not only that, it will also show your boss that you're committed to the company and are willing-to-learn more about what opportunities lie ahead.

4. After the in-depth conversation with your boss, agree on how to make it happen. Set an action plan and schedule to have it reviewed regularly. This way, you are making sure that things are being worked on towards the direction, and not a one-off conversation. It also means that when you completed the list of work, you can have some kind of expected progression which was previously agreed on.

5. Ask if they will provide you opportunities for career growth or put you in contact with the people who do have that power and authority over promotions, transfer, new projects and so on. If your boss says that there are no future positions available, ask them why not and what would it take for one to become open? For example,

"If I did this thing here (name a task) wouldn't that create an opening for me?"

6. Finally, keep track of all open discussions concerning any sort of career objectives. This will ensure that you log all conversation, which can serve as a reference along the way, and there won't be any surprises at the end when everything needs to come together as one.

Understanding how to have a successful conversation with your boss about career growth can be the difference between your career success and failure with the company. With the right moves, you'll set yourself up for future opportunities that will help grow your career.

How to Ask Your Boss for a Promotion

NOW THAT YOU ARE eyeing for the promotion to the role that is vacant. How to talk to your boss about a promotion? It can be hard, but it isn't impossible. You state your interest and ask them for one. Let them know how much you want this and what benefits they can get from promoting you. Point out how that one move will make their team or office stronger than before.

But before you do that, you need to prepare for the conversation. It's important for any employee who wants a promotion to know that they have been performing well at their current position for at least two years (a guideline) before asking for one. It is also important to consider if there are other people who have been in their position longer than you when evaluating promotions.

If you ask too soon or without good reason, it could seem like you are not satisfied with what you currently do and lack commitment. If this has been the case in the past, then it will be difficult to convince your boss that promoting you is worth their risk, time and energy when there are others waiting in line who may be more deserving than yourself of a promotion!

Some questions you might need to consider when asking for a promotion:

1. What are some reasons you feel ready now instead of waiting for another year?

2. What benefits will it provide the company and how will it benefit them in return?

3. How long do you have to stay at your role before you ask for a promotion?

Asking your boss for a promotion can be tricky. You need to know how and when to start the conversation, what you want from the role, and how to convince them you are ready for it. It's important to know how to ask for one the right way and when the time is right.

The more time you spend waiting, the less likely it will be that your boss will consider promoting you to the next level. For those who are confident in themselves and have been working hard, then now is as good of an opportunity as any! If there's something holding you back from taking on extra responsibilities or being promoted, then get clear with yourself about what those things might be so that when the time comes to talk to your boss, you're ready.

Once you are in the conversation, you need to convince your boss to promote you. If there are any obstacles in the way of a promotion, then they will need to be cleared. Some things that might get in the way include lack of funds, not enough time, or your boss doesn't think you are ready for that job scope. If these issues exist, then come up with some solutions so that when you talk about them with your boss, they can see how easy it would be! For example, if there is an urgent need to fill this new role but their qualifications don't match up exactly than offer yourself as a temporary option until someone better suited becomes available. This will give your boss an opportunity to assess you and reverse any impression they might have of you, while assessing your suitability for this new role.

What I'm saying here is that what may seem like a problem should also present itself as opportunity; use creativity and your initiative to proactively "make it easier" for your boss to promote you. Putting up anyone for promotion takes a lot of justification. This is especially true when there are many qualified contenders vying for the new vacant role. Instead, you will need to answer, "why me?"

If there are many candidates that share the same skill set as yours, look for a differentiating factor and offer it up without sounding arrogant. You may have more experience than others or hold some skills outside their comfort zone; these can be useful points when discussing why they should hire you over someone else. If this is not possible, focus on how well you understand the job requirements and show them what makes you stand out from other applicants such as extra qualifications in related fields or an impressive portfolio of work samples.

Your boss ultimate decision to promote the best candidate will solely be by their own evaluation and you can only do so much to help them with your input. Even if you missed this opportunity, save your discussions about moving until another day when there's another opening and more room on the team or budget to promote someone for the new vacant role. By showing that you're invested in what you do will also help pave the way for future promotions, as it shows how much potential they could see from promoting you if they made an opening available.

In short, so long as you prepare well and proactively pursue a promotion, your chance of quick progression is high. This is definitely a better alternative than passively waiting for the boss to notice you. However, take note that whilst working for a small company means that you have less competition, it's more difficult to climb the corporate ladder because the hierarchy organization chart is flat. Conversely, working at large companies is more of an uphill battle with many workers jockeying about for promotions!

How to Ask Your Boss for a Pay Raise

YOU'VE BEEN BUSTING YOUR ass at work, you're committed to the company, and you feel you are a great asset. So you think you deserve more money, and you don't want to wait for someone else to give it to you. There's no better time than now to asking for a pay raise. But wait, how can you talk to your boss about asking for a raise? Asking your boss for one can be nerve wrecking and in the end, they might not even believe that you deserve one. Your boss will most likely reject you until there's a compelling case justifying it. This means it must be clear to them on how much value and worth you bring to the organization.

How can you make them want to say yes to your request? All these questions cross your mind until finally it all comes down to one question: What is your merit for asking pay raise? It's actually easier than you might think- but there are some key points that will help get them on board with your request.

There are many ways how you can justify for your pay raise request. One of the best ways to ask for a raise is to first identify why you deserve it. For example, how much time and effort have you put in? How successful or productive are your projects and tasks? Are there any awards that show off your achievements? Despite what people might think about asking for more money, they're smart enough to know when someone deserves one, so if you can prove your worth (even before mentioning anything), then this will go on your favor as well.

Be prepared with supporting evidence when discussing qualifications; try using common phrases like "as I mentioned" or "I want to reiterate". Mention specifically which prominent project that you'd handled well recently. Start by reflecting on your achievements. One of the best things you can do at work that will increase your chances for a raise is contributing innovatively to projects or tasks assigned by managers. This shows them how much more value they are getting from you than if they just hired someone off the street with no experience! Showing initiative through innovation will show employees as being valuable assets worth investing in. Consider how your work has contributed to the success of an organization. It's a good idea to be as specific and detailed about what you've done, but it doesn't have to be long. You just want enough detail that they will see how valuable you are to them.

You can also do some homework and identify the criteria by which they judged success within the company. This means checking the company's website, reviewing market standard salaries through sites that do broad based industry wide statistic etc., so you'll be able to compare your salary with others' and close the gap if there's any.Once you have all this information, when to ask for a pay raise may be as simple as picking a right moment for asking your boss about salary and pay raise. It can be nerve wrecking if you're not careful- but it doesn't have to be! The best time to ask for one? It's when they are feeling generous, during the work review cycle, or after an accomplishment.

When you bring up the topic, you don't want to appear begging for more money. This will make them think you are greedy, which isn't always true. So how do you talk about your worth in a way that shows value without offending them? One of my favorite phrases is "I am here because..." This phrase helps establish why you deserve what you ask for, and that is the kind of input that they will need to have to evaluate whether they can afford more money for you.

Remember to always have a plan before the conversation. Be specific and be clear about how you much you want and how would like to see this happen. Your input should help your boss to justify your pay raise, that means it should give specific evidence of your accomplishments that make you worth what you ask- even if it's just anecdotal evidence!

When you discuss, act confidently and professionally. Prepare yourself for a high level of interest in order to convince them you have the knowledge, skills, experience and expertise necessary to perform at this higher level of salary. Always remember though - be confident but not arrogant!

Be ready to offer alternative solutions if they are hesitant about giving you more money. You can offer some ideas on how else they can compensate you instead (e.g., flextime). Showing initiative is key here as well as demonstrating an understanding of what's being requested from you while offering alternatives where possible. And one last very important thing is this - don't forget to negotiate salary and benefits packages in tandem so that you are always getting something better out of the bargain. After doing everything mentioned above, what can you expect? The worst outcome is that your boss will turn you down and keep paying the same salary. Remember, there's no guarantee they will say yes to your request.

Also, don't be surprised if the boss asks why, how much more money do you need or what have you done in comparison with other people in this company. Your preparation should help you answer those questions confidently. Asking for something without knowing its impact on one of their most valuable resources isn't wise.

In conclusion, the boss is not obligated to give you a pay raise. But if he sees the value of your contributions and knows that they are worth it, then the possibility will be higher. Never ask, never know!

How to Talk to Your Boss About Quitting

DO YOU FEEL LIKE the time has come for you to quit your job? If you're reading this with great interest, you probably have a looming conversation with your boss soon. It's hard to know how to talk to them about quitting when you want to resign from your job, and it can feel like a daunting task.

There are many reasons to quit your job, but there is one thing that will make the process easier for both parties: proper communication. It is important that you do it in a way that will not jeopardize your relationship with your boss. Especially so if you are working in a close-knit industry and you never know when you might cross paths again with your old employer or colleagues again.

But how do you tell your boss that you want to resign without burning bridges? How do you keep yourself in good graces with them before and after quitting? The best way to have the conversation with your boss is up front. You don't want them catching wind of it from another source and then having a negative reaction, or worse, finding out in some unfortunate manner—and this will happen if you wait too long! I'll break down the steps so you can have one more conversation with them and leave on good terms.

1. Offer your reasons you want to quit. You will definitely need a reason to why you are moving on, but don't give too many reasons

to explain why you want to quit either. You never know how they'll react after hearing it. They may take this personally or find out the real reason later on down the road and become resentful towards you when they learn more about the situation through colleagues. You need everything spelled out before going into this discussion with them so that there's no confusion left open between each other afterward.

2. Keep it short and simple and reach for a common understanding. If the reason you left was because of some internal conflicts within the company, you should not try to convince your boss that you're right or that they are wrong. The conversation should not come out to blame any party for your decision to quit the company. This is not the time for a long-winded explanation about how you feel your boss or company has wronged you, what with all their ills and woes. Keep your speech concise to prevent lengthy arguments that will only slow down the quitting process more than necessary.

3. This meeting can sometimes be uncomfortable and awkward, but it need not necessarily be. You could also just talk to your boss over the phone, but it will be easier for them to understand what you want if they see that you're serious about this decision.

4. Make sure there aren't any extensive projects or deadlines looming before quitting, so that's not another reason someone might think negatively of your leaving now (or if anything goes wrong).

5. Offer to help facilitate and smoothen the transition. In order to maintain a positive professional relationship with your employer, offer to help prepare your company and team for the impending departure. This shows that you genuinely care about what happens

in their success while also moving on from other opportunities available. You can strengthen these relationships by showing them how much they mean not only as friends but also employees of this company who work hard together every day.

6. Remember to express your gratitude. Thank your company and tell them you are grateful for their support as a mentor. It is important to express your sincere gratitude to them for all the opportunities that they have given you, all the effort that they had groomed you to become of what you are today, all ready to take on greater challenges.

Finally, it is important to know the right thing to say when you are breaking the news to your boss. I've compiled some of the most useful phrases that you can use to help ease the conversation.

1. I've been thinking about quitting for a while now. It will be good as it is time for me to start something new, but before I quit, could I ask for your advice?

2. There's an opportunity at another company that seems like a better fit, and if they offered the same salary package as I have here in place, I would take them up on their offer.

3. The hours or work balance don't align with my life goals and values anymore, so this is going to be best decision for myself and family.

4. I'm ready for my next challenge and I'm confident that this new opportunity will be the right fit for me.

5. I've learned so much from our time together and feel really grateful to be given the chance to take what I know here into another organization.

6. I think it would help us both if we could part ways on good terms, there's no hard feelings or ill will between us at all. It was just

time for me to move onto something else. 7. I have been incredibly happy at the company and I'm grateful for all that I've learned here; however, in order to take on new challenges (or some other reason), which means it's time for me to move on. Thank you so much for everything!

8. It was great working with each of you while we were together.

While you are darn sure that your departure is imminent, I feel that it's only right that I give you a last reminder to reconsider again and plan for what happens next. Make sure you know the timeline of when you want to leave and how long it will take before that can happen. If quitting is something that's been on your mind for a while now, make sure this isn't just a rash decision because if it doesn't work out like you hope, it may be difficult or impossible to get back into the workforce in the future. If this is your final decision, I will take this opportunity to wish you all the success and good luck in pursuing your goals elsewhere!

Personal Related Topics

HOW TO TALK TO YOUR BOSS ABOUT A PERSONAL ISSUE THAT PERSISTS AT WORK

IF you're in the middle of a personal crisis and are worried about how it will affect your job performance, then I have advice for you. If you've even been considering talking to your boss about this, there is already enough reason for you to do so. You may not think the problem is affecting your work performance, but just because you can keep it together on the surface doesn't mean that deep down inside you are doing well. There may also be some circumstances where what might seem like a private issue could eventually become harmful on the workplace - such as harassment - but either way, I recommend speaking with them before things go too far down that road.

It's always hard to bring up a personal issue with your boss, but it might be necessary if you have an issue that persists at work. It's this statement that many of us fear - "I need to talk to my boss about something." Sometimes it is because we are afraid. The conversation can be tough, but it may come to a point where inevitably, you will need to approach them. That is why I urge you to tackle it early, before it gets out of control.

But how do you prepare for the conversation? What are some things that might happen in the meeting, and how can you best handle them? It's important to be aware of how these issues can affect your workplace environment and what you need to say. When you feel you are ready to speak, ask for a private meeting with your boss. Find a good time to ask them for a date and time for a private discussion. This is crucial because you need to set your boss in a "receive mode" so they will be able to thoroughly listen to what you have. The easy opener is simply "can I talk with you about something" so there are no surprises.

Again, timing is everything to ensure an easier conversation. If your boss has a busy schedule, they will probably be more receptive if it's done earlier in the morning or during lunchtime breaks than later on in the day. This might also depend on their personality and how much patience and energy they have left for work-related matters at that time of day.

My advice is to prepare beforehand on how much details you will share with your boss. It's helpful to think about what level of disclosure is the right amount for them. For example, if you're feeling overwhelmed with a lot on your plate and need some help in prioritizing tasks or delegating responsibilities, then telling them about this might help get rid of any surprises down the road. If it's personal, such as an argument with a spouse or other family member that is affecting your performance, then it might be best to discuss this type of information confidentially after work hours.

Your boss needs to understand your problem because the more they know, the better able they will be to help you find a solution. However, be sure not to over-exaggerate or understate anything when talking with them, because this can cause miscommunication later on down the line. Understatement might make them think that there is nothing wrong, while overstatement could leave them thinking that the issue is a lot worse than it really is.

When you explain about the problem, it might be good to be as specific as you can about the situation like how much impact it has on your work, what you need to do in order to fix the problem, and how much time it will take? All this information is critical for them to assess the situation and help you find a solution. For example, your boss can recommend things such as therapy to address your personal issues if they don't think it will interfere with your performance at work. If the issue isn't fixable, there may be some other accommodations that they can offer which might also help, e.g. flex time or another work schedule. What you want to achieve here is to find a solution and not just a listening ear. Go directly to the point of potential impact and seek resolution. By the end of your discussion, you should clearly understand what's going to happen and how long it will take. Work on the proposed solution agreed between you and your boss, and keep the conversation going until you resolve the matter. Keep your boss updated with your progress and update them with any final closure.

To re-emphasize again, you do not want to just "suck it up" and work through personal issues that are affecting your performance at the workplace. It's important for you to feel comfortable enough discussing this with your boss as soon as possible, so you don't have unresolved feelings build up over time. Talking about your problems early on will allow you to address them in ways that won't affect your job negatively or take away from productivity during those days when life throws unexpected challenges your way.

HOW TO SPEAK WITH YOUR BOSS ABOUT WORK LIFE BALANCE

IF YOU SPEND TOO much time working without breaks or face difficulty in getting out the door for family obligations, then you should learn about managing hours. Trying to balance work-life balance is tough, and you're not the only one feeling it. Many of us are feeling the strain of trying to manage our time and responsibilities at work and home. I still struggle with that occasionally.

Work life balance can be difficult to achieve, with so many competing priorities. While you might want to spend more time at work because you are passionate about your career and you care about the company, you also need to take care of family members who depend on you.

It's hard to find enough hours in the day for both work and family. You have to clock the hours not only for productivity on the job but also for your mental health. If you have been struggling to balance time spent at work with time spent at home, then you should speak with your boss about managing hours so that you can find an equilibrium between work life and personal life.

Giving your boss a heads up can make the conversation easier. You could talk to them beforehand and tell them you are interested in finding a balance between work time and personal time and want their input on how best to do it. Of course, if you don't have this opportunity with your boss or they won't be receptive, just start by talking about what is going well at work currently before discussing other aspects of life outside of work.

If you have any brilliant ideas on how to do the same work in lesser time, or what activities you could do that would make your routine easier and faster, there is no reason not to share them with your boss! You may free up more time for personal priorities without compromising the quality of work.

Likewise, if you feel there are any tasks that take up too much of your time, but don't help the company meaningfully, then give ideas and suggestions for how to improve the task that will give you extra free time away from work while also helping the company. This is a win-win situation, and your boss is most likely to accept your suggestion to do things in your proposed way.

You can also consider a flexible schedule if your job scope allows it. You can explore the possibility of adding one additional hour to your usual working hours, so that you can have a half day schedule on your last working day. In an example, if you are working a typical 9-5 work hours and if you opt into a flex schedule from Monday to Thursday by staying only until 6 pm, then it can be possible that you will end your Friday at noon!

Another option might be to have a remote working arrangement, like working from home for one day per week. Research your job responsibilities and see if there's any task that you can rearrange so you can work from home. Once you come up with a proposed solution for this issue, present it to your boss and highlight the potential benefits like cutting commuting time and boosting productivity. If your boss isn't on board with the idea, offer to test it out for a set period before deciding if this will work in the long run.

If things go well during that time, you'll be happy and so will your company.

The better you are at communicating how your request can help improve the company's productivity and efficiency, the higher your chance of getting a flexible working arrangement that may help you achieve your goal of seeking your desired work-life balance.

How to Talk to Your Boss about Work Related Stress

WHEN IT COMES TO the workplace, stress is inevitable. You could have a demanding job, or your workload might be too heavy. Regardless of what's causing you stress at work, if you don't handle it well, then it will affect your productivity and performance. Many people refuse to talk about this because they worry that talking about their stress may jeopardize their livelihood but the more they bottle up their feelings, the worse the consequences will be.

It is important to take care of yourself and your mental health. It's your body's way of telling you that something has gone wrong, and it needs to be fixed. But when stress becomes chronic, the consequences can be severe, affecting your mental health and job performance. There are several things that you can do to help manage this stress. Work things out with your boss to resolve the matter together. This is especially important if your job belongs to the high-risk scope.

Talking about work-related stress is a sensitive subject, especially when you are not sure how your boss will respond. It is not always a straightforward task. But if it affects your job performance, then you must speak up. It can be a hard conversation to have, but you will learn how to have a successful conversation with your boss so they can help you reduce it and get back on track as soon as possible.

Here are a few tips you can try to ease your conversation with them:

1. Be honest with yourself and identify what's causing you the work stress. You probably know what's causing your work stress, so be honest with yourself. If you have a thousand things on your mind at once and they're all weighing down on you like a ton of bricks, then this may be the source of uneasiness for which to speak up about. You can do this by writing it down, so you don't forget to consult your boss about the issue.

2. Do not feel obligated to disclose everything. You can share what you want them to know. Instead of stressing out about what to say to your boss, just explain the sources of stress and seek advice on how to eliminate or reduce them. Be to the point and do what is needed.

3. Discuss what is making you stressed and the signs that it's affecting your performance at work. If you feel as though a certain project or task is causing more stress than usual, then chances are it has been for a while. However, if the latest development in such things like an added workload has caused increased stress levels, be sure to mention this.

All these will also help them understand where exactly your frustrations come from when mentioned specifically whether they're due to long hours on tasks that need perfection, difficult deadlines which make time management hard, or competition with others working towards the same goal can all lead to increased feelings of anxiety and frustration. And knowing these specifics may help them better decide how best to fix the problem.

4. The way you talk about your stress with your boss is not like talking to a friend. This meeting should be more direct and informal so that the topic can come up with no added pressure or

embarrassment on either end. If you have an open line of communication, this conversation will flow easier because there are fewer barriers between you both. It's important for bosses to understand what is going on in their employees' lives outside of work as well- after all, they're people too! And once again, understanding where the issues lie when tackling them could help ease some anxiety and frustration from both parties involved.

5. Be open-minded when discussing the work stress. Your boss's suggestion may differ from what you had initially thought, but never dismiss his suggestion just because it differs from yours. If you will try something new, it might surprise you with how much it can help you! Your boss might have fresh ideas on how to go about your stress relief, and it wouldn't hurt to hear him out before refusing his suggestion based on the unknowns of what he has in mind for you. Ultimately, your boss is fully responsible for your wellbeing at work and wants what's best for their employees. So adopt an open-minded attitude when discussing work related stress with your boss to ensure that both parties get what they want in this conversation.

I would like to nudge you forward to have a conversation with your boss today if you have been sitting on work related stress for a long time. It's never too late to get into the conversation today. The longer you wait, the more serious your consequences will be in the future! Many people worry about talking to their boss about stress at work because they are afraid it might put them out of a job. But this isn't always true because many bosses will want what's best for their employees and would never fire someone just because they felt stressed outside of work.

How to Talk to Your Boss About Your Work Anxiety

A VARIETY OF DIFFERENT things, such as workloads, deadlines, or even personal life events, can cause stress, while anxiety is typically triggered by one specific event that's causing you worry.

Many people who experience work-related anxiety may not even realize that they are suffering from an anxiety disorder. You need to know the difference between stress and anxiety, and it's important to understand what each one entails in order to cope with either. Once you know the difference, it will be easier to identify which type of feeling you are experiencing so that you can address it appropriately.

I've suffered from mild work anxiety in my earlier years of my career. I know what it's like to have sleepless nights because of the fear that you're not doing enough. You might be anxious about your current project, or you might suffer from an anxiety disorder and need help. A general solution for anxiety is to speak out. There are many forms of work that require a higher level of skills and experience in order to tackle the challenges more effectively. That means as you get more experienced in the job, the anxiety will eventually fade out.

Are you suffering from depression? Do you have to tell your boss about your mental health?

I know that's a hard question to answer. But the quick answer is, no. However, if you have this condition that is constantly making your work anxiety worse, it is likely you will need to tell your boss about them at some point.

I am fortunate enough not to have suffered from depression or an anxiety disorder, but I have friends who suffered from both. Talking with their bosses had helped to help them manage their work stressors and stay productive while maintaining good mental health. That is why it may be good to get all prepared and seek a private session with your boss as soon as you identify the condition, in order to help you relief the emotional stress.

Think about what you might need before you engage your boss. It's important to think about what you need, and not what the boss thinks will help. If a specific project or deadline that you're afraid of missing caused your work anxiety, then talk about this specifically. Can an additional team member help you? Can you take some time off to recharge your energy level, or will it help if your boss were to give you a more manageable deadline?

If the work anxiety is not so specific, then it's important to talk about how this issue affects your productivity. How long have you been feeling like this and what kind of effect does it have on other people in the office? Does anyone else suffer from similar symptoms that might be related to stress?

To help you have a better conversation with your boss, write about how you are feeling when a certain task is affecting your emotion. I had to keep a journal of my work and home life so that I can see what was triggering me. What you can try to find out is how did the anxiety manifest itself? Was it at certain times or places? Is there any triggers like being around people, deadlines, emailing clients about their problems while also trying to manage them yourself? Or are you always feeling nervous? Are your hands shaking ever so slightly, or are they still and clammy like a wet sponge? What is going through your head? Is it just one thought repeating over and over again in an endless loop of worries? Is it the fear that you won't be able to do this task adequately enough for somebody else's standards, not yours? Or does your mind go blank because there isn't anything left inside to give anymore? These are all things you need to reflect on when thinking about how you want help from your boss because they are not psychic. They don't know what's going through your head unless you tell them. Your boss may not be a doctor, but chances are they might know what your problem is because that certain task may have caused a common problem that they have seen in the workplace.

Try to be more open-minded about your boss' suggestion and be ready to try new things and don't forget that it's OK to have a different opinion. You may just need someone else's perspective on the situation to provide clarity for you to find peace with your decision. Sometimes talking about your worries reduces the anxious feelings that are bottling up in you. If your boss suggested another team member to help you with the project, don't feel that you are losing your position. It's not a sign of weakness but strength to ask for help when needed. If they suggested a short sabbatical leave, go for it because it's okay to take a break. That might be your what you needed!

Early intervention can help ease feelings before they escalate into major problems. Bringing up issues early also gives bosses an opportunity to find solutions that will reduce any unnecessary worry. The conversation may be a lot easier to handle than you think. You might also get some validation knowing that other people struggle with anxiety and depression too or maybe even just having someone hear what is troubling you will help make everything feel less overwhelming for a moment. It won't fix things immediately, but it gives you time to figure out how best to deal with those feelings while not feeling so alone.

In the extreme, if the entire job seems too much for you, it may be worth considering switching careers or looking for one that suits your skill set better. This also applies if all your current projects are causing stress; maybe taking on fewer assignments would ease some pressure?

How to Talk to Your Boss About Your Mental Health

FOR MANY PEOPLE, THE idea of talking to their boss about mental health is difficult. Many people have mental health problems, but often live with them in silence. However, it's important for you as an employee to be open and honest with your employer and make management aware if any aspect of your condition is affecting your job performance. If I have convinced you to seek help from your boss, then it's natural for me to show you how.

1. Use a private conversation and do not bring up this topic in a meeting or at work event to tell them and ask for their support. This is often the best option when you think that your boss may have some understanding or experience with mental health issues too or if not, they will probably be receptive.

2. Be honest and open about what you're feeling but again it's you who decide how much to disclose based on your comfort level. There is no need to go into a lengthy discussion of your medical history. You may feel embarrassed during the discussion, but remember that you are having this discussion because you needed help.

3. Speak to your boss about some changes you can make in order not to make the situation worse. This is effective when you've identified a trigger. Suggestion such as working from home or taking

a break from work could just be one of many ways how you might improve the condition. It's always good to be open-minded to your boss suggestion too!

4. Sometimes your boss can be rather helpless about the situation, especially if they have never been involved in such a situation. Let them know that even if they can't fix the problem, they can help make things better by providing support. Sometimes you want to voice it out to your boss just so they know why you are struggling, and an acknowledgement from them might do a lot for how you feel!

How to Talk to Your Boss If You're Struggling

TALKING TO YOUR BOSS about how you're struggling is never easy, but it's often necessary. Dealing with work difficulties can be challenging for anyone, but it is especially difficult when you are working and dealing with personal problems. Whether it's work, family problems, emotional issues or sudden emergency events that are causing the struggle, all these will affect your work performances or your current project that is soon missing the dateline.

How do you start this conversation? What can you, or should you expect from your boss in return? What if they don't take you seriously? You are probably already feeling overwhelmed, stressed, and anxious. You definitely do not want to create another stressor in cause your boss does not take it well when you talk to him about it. Yes, it's going to be another difficult conversation. But you can learn how to approach them for help without looking like a total liability.

First, you can assess your current situation and come up with a plan on what to do if things get worse. For example, if you are struggling with the current project that you are handling, think about what you can do so you can complete everything on time. Is there someone else who can help? How will it affect your current responsibilities if anything happens? What are some backup plans in case of emergency? Does this conversation need to happen now, or should you wait until things calm down a little more and get back on track first?

Once you are ready, schedule a private conversation with your boss and talk it out. If they are not the type of person who will take you seriously in a public space, ask for a private conversation in their office. Be clear and specific about your struggles and what they need to do to help. For example: You are at risk of missing deadlines because _____. How much effort would it take to complete on time? What resources do they need to provide to make sure everything in on run rate? When should they expect results if the request was granted? Be concise but don't sugarcoat either!

At this stage, they may ask about what's causing the struggles, because they need to be clear about it so they can rearrange your job scope if it's necessary. It really depends on how much you will disclose, but the more you do, the more precise the solution will be to tackle your short-term struggles.

If your struggle is due to work politics or something specific that happened at work, talk about how it made you feel and why it was upsetting so they understand where you are coming from. Or if you feel like there are larger issues going on in your workplace, consider asking for their advice about how to handle the situation. If they don't know either, it could be a good idea to have that conversation with someone else in management. This is the most cumbersome conversation because it doesn't involve just you, but might implicate other people in your company.

If it's more of a personal problem happening at your workplace, ask them for advice about how to handle it on a day-to-day basis. This might be as simple as asking for a change of team or a change of project.

If your struggle is with your health issues, you can start by stating that you are having a hard time with work and it might not be your fault. You don't need to mention specific details but just say how much of an impact this has on your productivity-both in quantity (amount) and quality (effectiveness). The more specific, the better. For example: "My doctor told me I needed surgery for my chronic condition X, or else I will have worse symptoms."

Your boss will then know that there is professional advice on your medical condition and that needs to be addressed. Most of the time upon hearing that it comes from a doctor, they are more likely to take you seriously, and may also refer you to HR for follow up solution.

If your struggle is with short term financial issues, sit down and have an honest conversation with your boss. Be clear about the time it should take for this issue to resolve itself or when you'll ask again. When asking them if they could advance some money, make sure to offer tradeoff in salary or more work hours over less pay.

You can figure out if there's a company policy that will grant short-term loans to employees who need financial help. I prefer this approach for two reasons. A loan from the company is helpful because it will be easier to repay than a personal favor, and you are not taking on any obligation or pressure that goes with it.

However, it's also possible that they will reject because even though they might say yes, what they really mean is "no". Think twice before accepting any offers of help from bosses who have been known not to follow through on their promises.

If your struggle is with family issues and you are riding an emotional rollercoaster, take time to explain the situation briefly to your boss and tell them you need additional time off for personal reason. Don't be afraid to ask for time off even if it's just an hour or two. This can help recharge your batteries and give yourself some space away from work. If they don't want to give you any, ask if there are other ways that can help like changing hours or days of work, etc. Don't make a big deal out of it because they might feel offended and think you're not committed to your job when the opposite is true.

Some tips you can do to help yourself when you struggle:

Take care of yourself by eating well, getting enough sleep, and exercising regularly.

Make your job more enjoyable by doing things like listening to music while working or taking a walk outside during lunch break.

Take a break when you feel overwhelmed or stressed out.

If your struggle persists, seek professional help from an outside source such as a therapist, counselor, or psychiatrist. Your boss can only so much to help you.

How to Tell Your Boss You're Unhappy at Work

IT'S IMPORTANT TO BE happy at work. How do you know when it is time to tell your boss that you are unhappy? There can be many reasons for this, and it could also depend on job scope. For instance, an employee might not be happy at work if they are assigned a new task or if they have to follow a new protocol created by the company. A new colleague who is constantly skiving may also cause some people stress at work and lead them to feeling dissatisfied with their current situation. When all these add up, it feels like every day at work is becoming more of an uphill battle than a chance to do something meaningful.

When you decide to speak with your boss about any dissatisfaction, do it constructively so as not to come across as hostile or ungrateful for opportunities already provided. It should be done to lead to a more positive experience in the workplace!

The first step is to identify the cause of your unhappiness. Is it a new co-worker? Is it a task that's been given more responsibility than you feel you can handle? Or is it an unreasonable sales target for the quarter? Write all your grievances and bring it to the boss. If there is something wrong with how work is conducted, or what goals are being set, make sure this issue sorted out with your boss.

When you're unhappy, it's normal to feel a variety of emotions and be irrational. This is the worst time to have a conversation with your boss. To prevent having an emotional outburst, it's best to vent to a close friend before talking to your boss. (that's what friends are for!)

Find out beforehand of what you could do about the issue and propose some solutions to your boss, discuss and agreed to a solution. This will show your boss that you're proactive in dealing with problems, and not avoiding them.

Learn to be mindful of your body language and tone of voice. Your body language should be open and not confrontational. It is important to monitor your posture and stand in a manner that is more inviting. The way you stand, and the hand gesture may unconsciously give off a different vibe to your boss. Your tone of voice is crucial when talking to your boss. It should not sound like total grievance or unhappiness with the company. You need to sound like there's hope for improvement in the future too!

In order to have a positive outcome for any such talk, it is important that any criticism, complaints or negative feedback are done out of concern and care for what you can do better going forward. In other words, try to focus on solutions rather than just problems as they arise. If you approach your issues from a more positive perspective than even if something doesn't work out, at least everyone will have tried their best, which often leads to an overall improvement in moods and feelings about the workplace.

How to Tell Your Boss You're Pregnant

FOR WORKING MOMS OR moms-to-be, one of your largest concerns is whether to announce your pregnancy at work. There is no correct answer, and this can be difficult to think about when you're busy with work or keep up socially in other parts of life.

Employees worry about how their boss will react when they hear the news, and that's understandable. The best way for you to handle this situation is by being as honest as possible; there may not be any "rules" but honesty always helps others understand what people are going through. Tell them in person when they are not busy, or call them and ask if they can chat privately about something important. This will allow you to prepare your thoughts so that there is less chance of feeling nervous while making this announcement.

I would recommend you let your boss know as early as possible so that they have time to make any necessary preparations for job changes in your short-term maternity absence. I listed below top 10 tips which I hope can help you when you are ready to share this splendid news with your boss.

1. Tell your boss as soon as you know for sure. If you're pregnant and when you are ready to announce to the world, the first thing to do is contact your boss and let them know the good news. This will give them time to prepare for any changes in workload that may occur because of your pregnancy.

2. Be prepared for questions about how far along you are, when the baby is due, or if you're planning on taking maternity leave. This will help them plan for personnel to cover your workload in your absence.

3. Be prepared for an initial negative reaction. Some bosses may be less than thrilled about the idea of having to cover maternity leave, but this doesn't mean they don't care. They may be worried about not being able to get the right personnel to cover your job scope without disrupting the workflow.

4. Offer to train someone who can temporarily step in when you're away and take over your responsibilities. Some bosses may be more open to the idea of having someone fill in for you if they know that person is good and will be well-trained enough to take over your duties.

5. Communicate with your boss throughout the process and be honest with them about any restrictions you may face. As your tummy gets bigger, you may no longer do certain tasks like how you had always been able to previously. A short-term change of job scope might smooth out some disruptions for their business while still giving you ample opportunity to contribute as an employee.

6. Share with someone close who knows how your boss may react before bringing up the subject at all. You want somebody else's opinion because nobody understands what goes on between two people better than those involved themselves.

7. Share the news with your boss in a way that will not appear aggressive or offensive. An example might be to say, "I have something important I need to share with you" and then follow up by explaining what they're about to hear, such as "I'm pregnant."

8. Explain why you are telling them now rather than later so when there is an opportunity for feedback, they can do immediately it instead of waiting until later, which may never happen. This also gives time for adjustments at work if necessary before the baby arrives.

9. Make sure the conversation is private and confidential. If you tell a coworker first, they may not keep it to themselves or share details with others, which can lead to rumors spreading quickly around the office.

10. Mention how your work has changed since becoming pregnant. For example, if you are more tired at work or have had less energy than usual recently this will show that there's been some change in your productivity levels because of pregnancy.

Finally, it's also worth mentioning that if you're thinking about asking for flex time, now would probably not be the best time; pregnant woman has extra needs like doctor appointments, which can make work more difficult. If you want flexibility with hours, then ask before announcing!

Closing Chapter

IN THIS LAST CHAPTER, I hope you have picked up enough valuable skills to at least survive the early years of your career. For those who have been in the workforce for a long time, I hope you find it useful when starting conversations with your bosses.

I'd tried to cover pointers and tips on how you can talk to your boss without feeling scared. I didn't list every scenario, but I tried covering the most common ones from what I have seen in my own experiences.

Do what works best for you and if that means talking one-on-one when the time is appropriate, do it! There is no right or wrong in the way of handling a conversation. Those pointers and tips can only bring you towards a direction, but because we human are all unique, it's difficult to predict with 100% accuracy how we will react to certain triggers. But following the advice should at least help you at the start.

Before we close the book on these chapters, I would like to recap the last few tips which I think are important.

1. The importance of talking to your boss with a calm disposition. Some bosses are just more sensitive and tolerate less than others, so be mindful of this when speaking to them.

2. To not take anything personally. More often than not you will misinterpret things said by your boss because it's just a result of how we process information in general. So always make sure you consider

all possible interpretations before jumping to conclusions or reacting emotionally.

3. To take a step back and consider things from the boss's perspective. Again, because we are all unique, it is important to understand where your boss is coming from before making any comments or assumptions.

I hope these chapters have been helpful for you who read it from cover to cover, or even just part way through! I'm hoping that with these pointers would give you an insight into some conversations which you have never thought about before. That's why I hope this book will be a useful resource for you to fall back on so that you will never feel afraid when you talk to your boss again.

END

Author Note

Do you like this book? What do you like about this book? Which are the tips that you find it most useful? How do you think other readers can benefit from this book? I'm reaching out to you because I know books can make a difference.

I wrote this book to share my knowledge with others who are struggling too, but don't know where to turn for help. It's been amazing hearing from people who have found the advice helpful, and I really want to continue making life easier for those in need of guidance.

If you could spare just a few minutes to read through my book and **leave an honest review** on the online bookstore where you purchased this book, that would be very much appreciated!

Your thoughts are important because they can help me write more books that will make a difference in someone else's life.

Thank you in advance for sharing your reviews with other readers.

Editor Note

Don't you wish you could read more books? Do you want to be the first person to know about new and upcoming releases from your favorite authors?

If you are a voracious reader who wants to read more books, then we have the perfect opportunity for you! The **Advanced Reader Team (ART)** is a program that allows our most dedicated readers to get free copies of upcoming books. It's also an opportunity to give us feedback and reviews on your favorite new titles. As an ART member:

1. You can get **FREE** copies of the latest books before they hit the shelves.
2. You also make a difference by giving feedback on how these books are received by future readers.

Learn more about ART program at:

https://sevensunsbookpress.com/about-artsi/